D1272365

R00196 10529

Finch, Karen

Caring for tex-
tiles

DATE DUE

FORM 125 M
Business/Science/Technology
Division

The Chicago Public Library

NOV 3 1977

Received

Caring for Textiles

Caring for
Textiles

KAREN FINCH O.B.E.

AND GRETA PUTNAM

Line drawings by Danielle Bosworth

Foreword by Donald King
Keeper of Department of Textiles
Victoria and Albert Museum

Watson-Guptill Publications   New York

To our husbands
Norman Finch and Leonard Putnam

© Karen Finch and Greta Putnam 1977

Watson-Guptill Publications,
a division of Billboard Publications, Inc.,
1515 Broadway,
New York,
N.Y. 10035

**Library of Congress Cataloging in
Publication Data**
Finch, Karen.
  Caring for textiles.

  Includes index.
  1. Textile fabrics—Conservation and
restoration.
I. Putnam, Greta, joint author. II. Title.
TS1449.F488   677'.02864'028   76-56462
ISBN 0-8230-0564-X

Printed in Great Britain
at the Alden Press, Oxford

Contents

Illustrations

Acknowledgements

We would like to acknowledge the help and advice we have received from our colleagues and friends in all our endeavours, with our special gratitude to Miss Anne Buck and Mrs Stella M. Newton.

We would like to thank the following individuals and institutions for granting us permission to reproduce objects in their possession: Michael Adda; Barlaston Church, Stoke-on-Trent; Dr Emile Boyd; Mrs D. Briscoe; Craven Estates; Irish Georgian Society; Mrs M. Law; National Maritime Museum; National Trust (Snowshill Manor, Uppark, Waddesdon Manor); Royal Albert Memorial Museum, Exeter; Royal Ontario Museum; Mrs Sluman; Charles Stewart; Victoria and Albert Museum.

We would also like to thank the following for use of photographs: By Gracious Permission of Her Majesty the Queen, pp. 74, 86, John and Pegaret Anthony, pp. 23, 82; Anthony Bock, pp. 14, 22, 30, 31, 75, 87; Barry Castelete, frontispiece, pp. 14, 22, 23, 23, 41, 48, 53, 73, 74, 79, 80, 81; Laurie Connon, pp. 18, 18; Stephen Cousens, p. 93; Chris Steele-Perkins, p. 76; Victoria and Albert Museum, pp. 74, 77, 86.

Foreword

Textiles are made to be used and, eventually, they become worn out and are discarded. But they can also be things of great beauty, historical interest or sentimental value, and in these cases it is natural that we should try to preserve them. This is not easy for, even if we protect them from the friction and soiling of normal use and the strains of repeated cleaning, they remain under continuous attack from their environment – from light which fades the dyes and weakens the fibres, from changing temperature and humidity which makes the threads work and twist as they take up and give out moisture, and from dirt and chemicals in the air which tend to destroy the fabric. As the authors of this book say, 'considering everything, it is a wonder that textiles survive for any length of time at all.'

Nevertheless, many do survive, sometimes for centuries, and there is a growing feeling that we should try to do more to ensure the preservation of fine old textilés. This feeling arises from a number of factors. The opening of the great country houses to the public has revealed the existence of many beautiful old textiles, some of which are in an advanced state of decrepitude. The increasing interest in collecting antiques of every sort has extended to the field of textiles and many of these, too, stand in need of conservation treatment. Also, many people who live surrounded by the myriad mechanically produced artifacts of the modern world have developed an understanding and respect for the beauties of hand-craftsmanship, and wish to employ their own handicraft skills to preserve old examples for future generations.

The present book, *Caring for Textiles*, will be an invaluable aid to all who are interested in this field. One of its authors, Karen Finch, trained in the Danish textile tradition, subsequently brought her skills to England and did remarkable conservation work on the textile collections of the Victoria and Albert Museum. Later she set up her own workshop, and in 1975 she became the first Principal of the admirable Textile Conservation Centre at Hampton Court Palace. Both her fellow-author, Greta Putnam, and the illustrator, Danielle Bosworth, have been her trusted associates for many years. They are all experts in textile conservation and their book incorporates their long experience and profound knowledge of the field. It is not, however, a manual for professional conservationists, but a practical guide for all those who own or are otherwise responsible for the care of old textiles. It examines all the questions which most frequently arise and provides straightforward answers in plain language. It lays down basic principles for protective housekeeping and gives detailed instructions for the treatment of the various categories of furnishing textiles, costume and so on. It describes clearly how to clean, repair and mount the various kinds of textiles. And it is particularly good in drawing the very important dividing line between, on the one hand, the kinds of cleaning and repair which can properly be undertaken by anyone with reasonable skills in washing and needlework and, on the other hand, the cases in which it is imperative to consult a professional conservationist.

I know, from the innumerable questions on this subject which have been addressed to me in the past, that this book fills a long-felt want. I shall certainly recommend it to future questioners, and I am confident that all who read it will find in it precisely the kind of advice that they require. It is a thoroughly practical guide and one which should do much to raise standards of care in the field of antique textiles.

Donald King
Keeper, Department of Textiles
Victoria and Albert Museum, London

Introduction

Over the years, we have been asked many questions about what can be done to care for textiles by those who own or have charge of them and who are aware of the importance of their preservation. We hope that this book will provide at least some of the answers.

It is certainly not intended as a textbook for those who wish to learn how to conserve textiles with a view to taking this up as a career, nor as a do-it-yourself book in the accepted sense of the term, but rather as a guide to those processes of display, storage, cleaning and conservation which we feel can be be safely undertaken by responsible people seeking to care for textiles. We have tried to explain the dangers and difficulties inherent in dealing with old, fragile and degraded materials and to point out some of the problems which can arise. The existence of these difficulties may not be suspected by those who are skilled in dealing with present-day fabrics.

Some readers may be collectors of embroidery, lace, costume or of dolls and fans or other objects with textile connections. The care of such collections may require specialist knowledge beyond the scope of this more general book and we hope that information will be sought through membership of an appropriate society or from the books we recommend.

Those who wish to do voluntary textile conservation work should seek out a group working under trained supervision. The National Trust, branches of the National Association of Fine and Decorative Arts Societies or the Embroiderers' Guild should be able to direct a volunteer to the nearest local group. The Textile Conservation Centre at Hampton Court Palace exists to undertake textile conservation and to train those who wish to do the work professionally. It is also able to give advice to individuals and groups, and runs day courses in preventive conservation for those in charge of textile collections.

Training for those who wish to make textile conservation a career is also given at the Centre in conjunction with the Courtauld Institute of Art to whom applications for particulars of the courses should be made. Museums with textile conservation departments accept trainees for museum work. Apart from a desire to do the work, a degree in a relative subject, for example, art history or chemistry, or an art school training with experience in textile construction and techniques such as weaving, provides a good basis for a training as a professional textile conservator.

CHAPTER ONE

Textiles and Fibres:
A General Survey

Think of your forefathers, think of your posterity! – JOHN QUINCY ADAMS

The term 'textile' can be used to cover a very wide range of objects. A large woven tapestry, hanging on the wall of a great house, is a textile but so is a delicate piece of lace. Clothes and many of the accessories worn with them, household linen and the so-called 'soft' furnishings such as curtains and upholstery are textiles, as are embroideries of all kinds, carpets and rugs, flags and banners, church vestments, altar frontals and many other church furnishings. The list becomes even longer if we also include objects such as dolls, parasols and fans, of which textiles are a part.

A history of textiles is virtually a history of civilisation, for man, all over the world, has made textiles from earliest times: nets to catch food and fabrics to cover himself for warmth, decoration and visual enjoyment. It is not known exactly when man began to weave but there are cave pictures from about 5000 B.C. which show primitive looms. Greek and Roman writers have described, with admiration, Babylonian tapestries which, they said, depicted rich garments, heavily embroidered and interwoven with gold. This would have required weaving of an advanced and sophisticated kind. Although these Babylonian tapestries have not themselves survived there are wall-paintings and decorations on pottery which show that even everyday clothes of the time were decorated with patterns in different colours. Balls of coloured wools, dating back to 2000 B.C., were found around the turn of this century by Sir Flinders Petrie in Egyptian tombs, and burial clothes have been found by other archaeologists in graves as far apart as Scandinavia and Peru.

Very few ancient textiles have survived and those which have were,

for the most part, found in tombs. The Egyptian tombs in particular had conditions very favourable for the safe-keeping of textiles, namely, cool and dark with an even temperature and humidity and unpolluted air. Apart from the occasional graverobber, the textiles would have been undisturbed for centuries. Some of the burial garments unearthed from tombs disintegrated on exposure to outside conditions but others have survived to find their way into museums and collections.

During the Middle Ages, textiles, particularly tapestries and bed-hangings, were of such importance that they were always put at the head of the list of valuables in wills and inventories. Many of the earliest textiles which have survived in this country are tapestries, which have always been very costly and therefore treasured, and ecclesiastical embroideries which again were valuable because of the materials used, including gold and silver. The latter survived also because of the care they received from Church or religious orders to which they belonged.

From the twelfth to the fifteenth centuries, England was famous all over Europe for embroidery of remarkable beauty. Known as Opus Anglicanum – 'English work' – this embroidery used materials of great value, particularly gold and silver thread, and the design and work-manship was of the highest quality. The output of the workrooms, staffed by professional, for the most part male, embroiderers who had served a seven-year apprenticeship, was sold by merchants who made this their special trade. Most of the embroideries were of religious subjects and were sold to churches for the decoration of vestments. Opus Anglicanum is mentioned no less than 113 times in a Vatican inventory of 1295. Embroidery was also done by nuns and there is a record, dated 1271, of an altar frontal for Westminster Abbey which had taken four women four years to complete. Quite a number of examples of Opus Anglicanum have survived and can be seen in museums, with perhaps the best known being the famous Syon Cope at the Victoria and Albert Museum in London.

For many generations, English gentlewomen were taught to embroider as part of their education. Some great houses employed professional designers and embroidresses, and ladies at court and in great houses and castles throughout the land spent many hours at their needlework.

In other ways, too, the history of Britain is closely connected with textiles, and those which have survived to the present day are part of its heritage and need our care and protection if they are to give pleasure and knowledge of the past to those who come after us.

FIBRES

All textiles are made from fibres which can be animal, vegetable or man-made. These fibres might be matted together to form a material in the way that wool can be matted to form felt, or they might be pulped with water and then beaten out into a cloth, as the Indonesians do with the tree-bark fibres from which they make tapa-cloth. More familiarly, fibres can be spun into yarn and the yarn can be fashioned into lace, knitted or crocheted, made into net, or knotted into trimmings and decorations as in tatting or macramé. But, most common of all, fibres can be spun into yarn and woven on a loom to make a fabric.

The properties and characteristics of the fibres from which a textile is made will always play some part in its reaction to the treatment it receives and the environment in which it is kept. Textiles made earlier than the middle of the nineteenth century were almost certainly constructed from natural fibres. These fibres are not, of course, designed by nature to be made into fabrics but have their own natural functions and, because of that, they will always retain some of the characteristics required to fulfil those functions, even though man has taken the fibres and used them for his own purposes by treating them, spinning and dyeing them and weaving them into material.

Wool

Wool is, by nature, intended to keep the animal on which it grows warm and dry, and it will, even when spun and woven into a material, still retain the ability to absorb up to one-third of its own weight in water without feeling damp to the touch. Indeed, wool needs an atmosphere in which there is a certain degree of moisture if it is not to become hard, dry and brittle. In their natural state, wool fibres are elastic and spring back after being stretched. Woollen material, too, resists being pressed into sharp folds and tends to spring back again. For instance, permanent pleating of woollen material, like permanent waving of human hair, can only be achieved by irreversibly damaging the cell structure of the fibres of wool and hair.

Wool tends to decompose under the action of strong sunlight and reacts unfavourably to heat but it will last and store well in favourable conditions. Apart from sunlight and dry heat, wool is liable to be attacked by moths and mildew and, because of their cell structure, wool fibres shrink and mat together if washed and rubbed in hot soapy water. With care, however, wool will wash successfully.

Wool does not burn very readily but if it comes into contact with a naked flame, its fibres decompose, giving off a smell similar to that of feathers burning. If the flame is removed, the wool does not continue to burn, but each fibre forms a black charred knob. This characteristic can be used to identify wool.

Silk

Silk is a natural thread which is spun by the silkworm, *Bombyx mori*, into a cocoon to protect itself while a pupa and from which it eventually emerges as a moth. Silk fibres are slightly less elastic than wool but, because they are so long, smooth and fine, they can be woven into a soft, luxurious material which drapes and hangs in beautiful folds. In manufacture, the gum-like sericin which holds the silk threads together in the cocoon is removed from the natural silk and this loss may be replaced in various ways, sometimes with metallic salts which produces 'weighted' silk. This presents problems in the care of silk material, especially if the amount of weighting is considerable as was often the case in black silk or silk used in the making of fringes or tassels. Weighted silk can seldom be successfully washed. Sunlight and hot dry conditions cause silk, especially weighted silk, to become dry and brittle but pure silk and good quality silk embroidery threads have longer lasting qualities. If silk comes into contact with a flame, it will burn, giving off a similar singed smell to burning hair or horn.

Linen

Linen is made from fibres which originally held the stems of the flax plant upright and carried moisture up from the roots through the plant to the leaves and flowers. Linen fibres, produced from the retted stems of the flax plant, even when woven into cloth, will always attract and carry moisture along themselves. Linen is always stronger when wet than when dry, and washes well and can be dry-cleaned.

Cotton

Cotton fibres come from the seed heads or bolls of the cotton plant. It has a greater resistance to heat than most other fibres and can be kept in storage for a long time without deterioration. Sunlight causes gradual loss of strength in cotton and yellowing of white cotton fabrics. Cotton fibres, like linen, are stronger when wet than when dry and, indeed, humidity is necessary when weaving cotton as anyone who knows the traditional cotton-weaving industry of Lancashire will testify. Cotton burns very readily if brought into contact with a naked flame. It can be dyed successfully but dyeing other vegetable fibres, especially linen, has not always been easy. Cotton is fairly resistant to solvents and generally will dry-clean successfully.

Man-made Fibres

Man-made fibres fall into two main groups, depending on the origin of the materials used to make them. There are those fibres made from materials with a natural origin such as cellulose or protein, and rayon is an example of a material made from fibres in this group. The other consists of synthetic fibres made from simpler substances, and polyester materials and nylon are examples of this group.

Identification is not easy and man-made fibres are now so numerous and varied that it would be impossible to do more here than advise that one should determine the characteristics of each before choosing one to use. Fortunately many, even bought from the roll, have quite good descriptive labels regarding care and treatment. This information is essential. Some will dry-clean successfully and others will not, most are washable, some are more flammable than others, some have the advantage of being stable and resistant to light but some are adversely affected by heat. Most of them are chemically inert and will generally combine quite successfully with natural fibres. Those man-made fibres which are known to have stable qualities and good resistance to light are frequently used in conservation as supporting materials.

By being aware of the characteristics of fibres, care can be taken in choosing materials for new work and also in deciding on the most suitable methods of cleaning and conservation of old fabrics. The nature of the fibres used must always be considered in assessing how materials could react.

DETERIORATION OF TEXTILES

All textiles start to suffer from deterioration from the moment they are made. There are many reasons for this apart from ordinary wear and tear to which, of course, very precious or special textiles would not be subjected to any great degree.

The greatest enemy of all textiles is light – not only visible light but also the ultra-violet radiation in daylight and that emitted by fluorescent tube lighting. Light causes not only dyes to fade but can also cause deterioration in the structure of the fibres themselves.

Another enemy to textiles is atmospheric pollution and, despite clean-air zones, the sulphur dioxide content in the air continues to harm textiles in industrial and urban areas and all other places where vehicles still emit their destructive fumes. Any kind of dust and dirt can harm textiles, particularly if the dirt contains gritty particles which can work their way into fabrics and cut the fibres.

Excessive dryness and heat, damp which can rot fibres or cause mould to grow, pests such as moths, chemical reactions set up by the constituents of stains and starches and their interaction with each other – all these can attack fibres and weaken them.

Up to now we have mentioned external conditions but a textile can have inherent weakness caused in manufacturing which might result in destruction. Some dyeing processes, although achieving the desired shade, will weaken and eventually cause the destruction of fibres. An example of this is the rotting by oxidation of the dark-coloured wools in tapestries. Before the existence of chemical dyes, iron was used as a mordant to obtain dark colours, particularly black and brown. Restoration work has shown that the dark outlines in the design, typical of Gothic tapestries of the sixteenth century, had had to be renewed on several previous occasions. But recent conservation replacement of these outlines, so vital for the proper visual appreciation of the design, with wools dyed by modern methods should ensure that replacements will not be needed so frequently in the future.

The detrimental effects of dyeing methods does not apply only in the case of old textiles. Starch dyes may well have been used on some of the present-day textiles which holidaymakers bring as souvenirs from abroad. The bright and beautiful colours which attract the travellers could disappear or run if the materials are washed, kept in humid conditions or exposed to light and therefore they need to be kept clean, dry and in the dark if they are to survive.

The late eighteenth and early nineteenth centuries saw a transition as far as dyeing was concerned because the earlier *natural* dyes were being replaced by chemical dyes. A great deal of experimentation took place and, consequently, the dye-stuffs used were not always completely successful. Some were so fugitive that they would 'bleed' their colour into surrounding areas just by exposure to damp atmosphere, let alone if the textile was put in water. There is one green colour, very much used for embroidery silks, which is a great culprit in this respect. We remember a beautifully embroidered man's silk waistcoat which had obviously never been worn but had unfortunately been stored in damp conditions and almost completely ruined because of this particular colour running. On a piece of canvas-work embroidery, a brown dye had actually rotted the fibres of the canvas on which the embroidery was worked, to the extent that the parts embroidered in brown had fallen out, although leaving enough traces to show the reason for the disintegration. We find it interesting, from an historical point of view, that aniline dyes seem to have been discovered before the man-made materials on which they are most effective and permanent. Aniline dyes began to be used about the middle of the last century on various textiles, but it may be that their true potential has not yet been realised and they may have more affinity with man-made fibres now being perfected than they had on natural ones on which they were apt to fade and change.

Manufacturing processes or finishes, too, can do long-term harm as a result of distortion or chemical treatment of the fibres even though, when new, the material was attractive and pleasing. An illustration of this is the weighting of silk previously mentioned. The natural gum-like sericin is removed from the silk during the processes of manufacture and results in the silk having less body or 'weight'. This can be replaced by metallic salts. It is likely that 'weighting' of some kind has been known from the beginning of the silk industry in China and a small amount of the weighting agent may not appreciably affect the lasting qualities of silk whether woven or used for embroidery. However, from about 1870, weighting began to be done in excessive fashion. Although some companies did little or no weighting of the silk they produced, one firm stated in 1909 that coloured silks could be weighted to between fifty and one hundred per cent and black silk up to four to five hundred per cent. For heavy weighting, the silk could be kept for days in a bath with tin or iron salts. Garments made of new weighted silk had the scroop, or rustle in movement, which was so fashionably desirable, besides having a heavy and expensive feel. Fringes and tassels, too, hang much better if the silk from which they are made has been weighted.

Weighting makes silk more susceptible to damage from light and, over a period of time, the weakened fibres of weighted silk tend to split and break, especially along the folds and hems where there is already some stress. These splits are indicative of a general weakness all over the material and it is very difficult to do anything to save it. Other dressings and manufacturing processes may also hasten deterioration whichever fibres have been used. Silk, in particular, has always been subjected to many different finishing processes.

If two different fibres are woven together into a material, one may actually contribute to the destruction of the other. Although both wool and silk will tolerate a degree of moisture, and indeed, as we have seen, wool actually needs moisture to survive, silk will rot if allowed to remain damp. A material, therefore, woven with a mixture of silk and wool yarns may look and feel most attractive but it will not last long in damp conditions – the woollen fibres will hold the moisture which will rot the silk.

CONSERVATION OF TEXTILES

Considering everything, it is a wonder that textiles survive for any length of time at all, and yet Britain is particularly rich in textiles of importance, some of considerable age. Many, of course, are in museums where they can be kept in controlled conditions and, as more is known and understood about how the textile should be kept and about conservation methods and techniques, this should ensure that they are safe for future generations to see and study. Other textiles are in more open conditions, many in great houses, often in the very surroundings for which they were originally made. Their future is less certain and safe but there is an increasing awareness of the dangers and an acceptance of the responsibility for their future safety on the part of those who have to care for them. Still other textiles are in private ownership valued as family heirlooms or purchased because they appealed as decorative objects or as additions to a collection. There may be others packed away, only half remembered or even forgotten. A textile does not need to look old and worn to need care. Prevention is always better than cure and preventive conservation is an important and positive way to ensure that a treasured piece in good condition will remain so whether it is on display or in storage.

If a textile requires treatment of any kind, then it will be necessary to decide who should be entrusted with the work. This is the first and most important decision to be made. If the textile has historic or artistic importance or is valuable in any way, then only an experienced textile conservator should treat it. So much can go wrong, and treatment by a well-meaning but inexperienced person could do irreparable harm. 'If only' are such sad words and a mistake in judgement or method is so easy to make if one does not have knowledge and experience. With something irreplaceable one does not get a second chance.

How can anyone decide if a piece is important? Its history may, of course, be known already, but, if not, the owner should find out as much about it as possible. Research could first be done at libraries, local museums or branches of the Embroiderers' Guild. Or it can be taken or sent to the Victoria and Albert Museum for appraisal. It is advisable to write or phone first for an appointment: the department to contact is the Textile Department or, if the piece is Oriental, then the Far Eastern or Indian Department, whichever is applicable. They will want to know what the textile object is – embroidery, costume, a piece of canvas-work, woven tapestry, lace or whatever – so that the appropriate expert will be seen who will be able to give information about the textile, its use and date and its importance but will not, of course, be able to value it. The museum does give a postal advisory service but that means sending the textile by registered post and there is always a delay of about a month before it is returned so, obviously, a visit is preferable. If a valuation is required, then application should be made to one of the well-known auctioneers and valuers. If someone owns a collectable piece and wishes to sell it, then it is best to do so before it receives any treatment so that the new owner can decide whether he wishes it to be conserved or restored and to whom he will take it for treatment.

A piece does not have to be spectacular to be important, but its age, and the rarity of its kind, may give it historic or artistic significance.

An increasing number of caring people are offering to help save the textile treasures of the past. There are voluntary schemes to do this but this work should always be done under constant trained supervision, not only for the safety of the textiles but also for the peace of mind of the volunteers. Most voluntary schemes are set up to work in situations where there are a number of important objects and, if mistakes are made, then something quite unique and irreplaceable may be irreparably harmed. If an object is damaged, the result is the same whether the damage was intentional or is the result of well-meaning but wrong treatment. The harm of such an occurrence would be twofold – the damage to the object and the guilt which the person who so unwittingly caused it must feel. Worse still, damage in this context may not come to light for some time. This is especially true in the case of some cleaning agents which give spectacular early results but may have long-term detrimental effects. However, provided there is always a trained conservator in charge who can explain and, with knowledge and integrity, guide the work of the volunteers, then they can certainly make a valuable and safe contribution to an urgent problem.

There are still some quite important textiles around, not all of them immediately recognisable as such, and perhaps a few examples of previously unknown but valuable pieces which have come our way may be of interest.

The first was two orphreys, pieces of ecclesiastical embroidery in silk and metal threads closely covering a linen background, which were brought to us for cleaning. The first piece in the form of a cross was rather out of shape and the other, a straight piece, showed some signs of wear. Otherwise, except for being dirty, they were in good condition. We felt that they were of an early date, even though they had, we were told, been recently removed from a vestment of purple Victorian velvet, possibly the last of many vestments they had decorated.

The Victoria and Albert Museum confirmed our assessment and identified them as examples of Opus Anglicanum, dated about 1425, and the experts were even fairly certain from their style in which professional workshop they had been made. The quality of the materials used was, of course, excellent as would have been expected from professional work of that time. This, and the fact that the pieces had been revered and therefore handled carefully, had undoubtedly contributed to their survival in such good condition. The small amount of damage on the straight piece had probably happened because that piece had been used to decorate the front of the vestment and had therefore been subjected to rubbing when the priest's garment had brushed against the altar, a common cause of damage to altar frontals and the fronts of vestments.

Cleaned and straightened, with the laid goldwork background gleaming softly and the silk embroidery showing the delicate shading of the saint's robes and the moulding of the figure on the cross in the centre, there was no question that here was something beautiful and of artistic as well as historic importance. Nothing was taken from or added to the pieces and no attempt made to *mend* it. Responsible conservation seeks to save what is there and neither adds to nor takes anything away from the original. The orphreys are now kept safe in a museum with a controlled environment, to be enjoyed as fine examples of the English work known and renowned as Opus Anglicanum.

The second example was a piece of embroidered linen brought to us for cleaning, mounting and framing. It was about fourteen by ten inches, a piece of coarse linen on which animals and insects were embroidered in tent stitch. The piece was dirty and some of the threads of the linen background were broken. The animals and the insects were placed in a haphazard fashion, rather widely spaced, and with no apparent attempt at a balanced design. Nevertheless, the piece had an artless charm which had prompted the owner to buy it from a stall at a church fête. Research showed that its date was about 1600.

There are samplers of Elizabethan work with similar embroidered animals or insects where a snail or a butterfly are the same size as a frog or even a lion, as if they were all felt to be of equal importance. But in samplers the placing of the animals does have a balance and design and generally they are quite close together. Elizabethan needlewomen often applied motifs, already embroidered on linen or fine canvas, on to rich background materials. Any visitor to Hardwick Hall in Derbyshire will have seen examples of this and it could be that sometimes these motifs were sold already embroidered. Whether this piece was an example of such work we do not know, but it is an interesting theory. The piece itself was washed, supported on to another piece of linen, made safe, mounted and framed. It looked charming. There is still research which could be done on it but, again, nothing has been added or taken away and if, at some future date, someone wishes to find out more, the owner has an up-to-date report on our findings and what has been done in the way of treatment.

Other 'finds' were items of dress bought by a collector without any initial excitement. The first was a petticoat which was dated about 1740 and which, at first sight, seemed not very different from others of the period. It was made of quilted cream satin in a very pleasant design. Examined in more detail, however, there was found to be no seam stitching the lining in place between the top part of the petticoat, which was fitted into the waistband, and the quilted part below. Closer examination revealed that the garment was made up of several widths of a doublewoven fabric, joined together with vertical seams. The top part of each width was made of the two weaves 'tied' together into a single layer of material. In the lower section the two weaves were only joined in the outlines of the design and the quilted effect had been achieved by the weaver adding a filler weft of padding in the course of weaving. This method of producing a material which had only one thickness for that part of the petticoat nearest the waist and hips while the lower part of the garment was padded for warmth, must have made

the petticoat very flexible and comfortable to wear and very warm, too. This example of doubleweaving including padding is, as far as we have been able to ascertain, unique in this country. The petticoat was carefully photographed and documented and will continue to be of great interest to both weavers and students of the history of costume.

The last find concerned two pairs of blue and white striped trousers, eventually identified as early and rare examples of sailor's uniform of the period of the Napoleonic wars. Ordinary working clothes, indeed the clothes of ordinary people, are seldom found in costume collections for many reasons. Made initially of materials of inferior quality, such clothes are usually discarded when worn out or else cut down for other uses and thus seldom survive. Uniforms for ordinary seamen are comparatively recent. Naval ratings originally had to supply their own working clothes but these trousers were probably specially provided and they are, therefore, historically important. One pair is now in the National Maritime Museum and the other in the Royal Albert Memorial Museum in Exeter. The trousers could not be dated with absolute accuracy but even that might have been possible had we known in time that the chemical composition of tar had been changed at a certain date. The trousers had unsightly tar marks which were removed but, had they been analysed first, this might possibly have helped to date the trousers a little more closely. The removal of stains from historical textiles is not always a wise or proper course to take, apart from the possible damage to the old textile. The ethics of responsible conservation hold that nothing of the original shall be removed and nothing added unless it is necessary to make the object safe or visually understandable; but stains, if they can be removed safely, are not generally left unless they themselves are important. Thus, bloodstains on garments of an historically important person should not be removed.

The examples we have given of textiles which were proved to be important can, of course, be matched by others where, far from geese turning into swans, the opposite was the case.

A canvas-work panel worked in *gros-point* and *petit-point* was acquired at auction and brought for treatment. It certainly had the appearance of a seventeenth-century piece and the new owner was delighted with her bargain. Close examination of the canvas and wools, however, pointed to a French nineteenth-century origin, although the style and subject was seventeenth-century. It was impossible to prove conclusively without lengthy research whether it was a copy or just an example of something done in an earlier style. The materials were not very good and the work necessary to make it safe made it very much less of a bargain than had at first seemed the case, although it was, as it had been at first sight, still a pleasant piece of work.

Our last example concerns a fairly large framed tapestry which had hung for many years in the bar of an inn. It had gradually become very dark in colour from the tobacco smoke in the atmosphere until a visitor, viewing it through the haze, suggested that, as it appeared to be of a very fine weave and in good general condition, it might be valuable and should be cleaned.

It was brought for treatment and proved to be not, as the owners had hoped, a fine handwoven woollen tapestry but a very good, cotton, machine-made imitation. Imitations of both woven tapestries and canvas-work embroideries were very effectively machine-made in the nineteenth century and they are important as a tribute to man's ingenuity rather than his artistry. We explained this and also the fact that, as dry-cleaning would have made little or no improvement to its appearance and, thus, it would have to be washed, the piece would almost certainly shrink, being cotton and not wool, and it would then need a new frame as the original one would be too large. The owners decided not to have the work done and it is quite possible that they put it back on to the pub wall to grow darker and more mysterious as time goes on.

Caring for textiles means having a responsible attitude towards them and, if the textiles are of importance, they should be given only to an expert for treatment. This may be expensive but, even from a purely mercenary point of view, will be well worth it. If research and expert assessment reveals that the textile is hardly a national treasure, however much it means to the owner, then that may justify the owner deciding to undertake any necessary treatment personally. The first step should be to record the results of research and advice and later to record any treatment given, and keep this documentation safely.

If a professional undertakes conservation or restoration work, the owner should have a detailed report accompanying the textile when it is returned. This documentation is important should anyone have to treat the textile in the future. Exactly the same sort of documentation should be kept by any person or group undertaking textile conservation, together with the results of any research undertaken and a photographic record of work done.

CHAPTER TWO

Display and Protection

The stately homes of England,
How beautiful they stand! — FELICIA HEMANS, *The Homes of England*

If one possesses, or has in one's care, something beautiful and visually satisfying, then it is natural to want to look at and enjoy it and, of course, allow others to share that pleasure. This can be achieved by putting the object in an accessible position and, one would think, in a good light. But, if the object is a textile, a great deal of further thought is required. Light, especially its ultra-violet radiation, is harmful to textiles, causing fading of colour and alteration in the structure of the fibres which results in disintegration, as we know by observing how quickly the material of curtains at a sunny window can deteriorate. Obviously then, the amount and intensity of light in the place chosen for the display of the textile will be of the greatest importance.

LIGHT

The international unit of illumination is the lux. In Britain in summer, direct sunlight out of doors could measure as much as 100,000 lux and the measurement on a dull day, inside, would be about 600 lux. From a conservation point of view, the advocated illumination for textiles is no more than 50 lux. Obviously in the open conditions of a house, as opposed to the more controlled ones of a museum, some compromise regarding the exposure of textiles to light must be achieved, but very fragile pieces should always be displayed where light can be excluded whenever it is possible to do so. These pieces should always be kept well away from direct light with, possibly, a well-placed source of artificial light for occasional use, remembering that artificial light can also cause

26

damage. Filters for absorbing ultra-violet rays can be obtained either as a sheet or a varnish for application to windows. Ordinary electric light bulbs and tungsten incandescent lamps are safer than fluorescent lamps which should be avoided as these emit ultra-violet rays unless filters are fitted.

PROTECTIVE HOUSEKEEPING

There are other ways to show care for textiles on open display. Valuable lessons can be learned from the way that the good housekeeping techniques of the past have preserved textiles in many of the great houses of Britain, now open to the public, where tapestries, curtains, bed-hangings, furniture and carpets of great age can still be seen, often in the very surroundings for which they were originally made. Certainly many of the houses are situated in the clean air of country parkland, away from the air pollution of industry, but that alone would not have been sufficient reason for the survival of the textiles, although it would have helped. Far more important is the treatment that the textiles and, indeed, all the contents of the houses received.

It was customary for the staff to be instructed to keep the furniture fitted with loose covers even when the family was in residence, and we know from eighteenth-century writers that these covers were removed only for the visit of someone of the greatest importance. Treasured bed-hangings had their own sets of protective covers, entire carpets were normally protected by coverings of baize or drugget, or strips of drugget were laid over those areas of carpet where the greatest wear could be expected. Even in quite humble homes, strips of hardwearing floor covering were laid over parts of the carpets to 'take the tread'. It was also the general custom, in both great and ordinary houses, to draw the blinds of all windows against sunlight, especially those of important rooms, to save carpets, covers and furniture from fading. In a great house, when the family were not in residence, everything was protected. Drugget was laid over all the carpets, dust-sheets covered the furniture and the blinds were drawn down.

Protective housekeeping of this kind is textile conservation in its simplest and most effective form. It meant, of course, that the owners of those beautiful textiles rarely enjoyed their possessions and one must hope that they were satisfied with the pride of ownership and the knowledge that they could, if they wished, gaze upon their treasures at any time. By their care, they have left a very important record of how great houses were furnished and decorated. Unfortunately, even before many of the houses were opened to the public, it had become difficult for subsequent owners to maintain those early high standards of care because of the dwindling number of staff available, and many of the textiles had already begun to suffer.

The presence of visitors in large numbers can contribute substantially to the deterioration of textiles and deterioration is a process which accelerates very rapidly. Opening a house to the public means subjecting the contents to increased exposure to light and to constant changes in temperature and humidity, all of which harm textiles. Those responsible for the care of the contents of such houses have a very real problem in trying to achieve a fair balance of interests so that visitors may enjoy the textiles without making too great a contribution to their destruction.

But even allowing for the fact that visitors will wish to see the textiles, there are still some safeguards in the way of preventive conservation which can be taken. Blinds should always be drawn down and the light excluded in every possible way when there are no visitors. Even when the houses are open, it is possible to cut down the amount of light, particularly sunlight, which is allowed to enter the rooms while still allowing sufficient illumination for the rooms to be viewed in comfort; in fact, many objects can be seen better in a subdued light. The human eye is very adaptable and, providing the change is gradual, can see in a surprisingly small amount of light. It would be possible, therefore, to decrease the amount of light available as the visitors proceed along a defined route through the house, say towards a corridor with no daylight at all. Here, fragile textile objects could be displayed in conditions where the minimum amount of artificial light was available for adequate viewing without causing visual discomfort or a feeling that the lighting was inadequate. Some museums solve the problem by using low general lighting and intermittent spot-lighting, again of surprisingly low power, so that very precious and fragile objects are exposed to the least possible light, and this method could be employed to some extent in other situations.

ATMOSPHERIC CONDITIONS

I durst not laugh for fear of opening my lips and receiving the bad air.
— SHAKESPEARE, *Julius Caesar*

A constant temperature of thirteen to fourteen degrees centigrade, with a relative humidity of fifty to sixty per cent is considered ideal for textiles. Unfortunately, little can be done to eliminate the fluctuations of temperature and humidity in a house open to the public without incurring prohibitive expense as well as altering the general setting. Putting individual items or groups of items into air-conditioned display cases for safety could alter the appearance of the rooms and create the feeling of being in a museum rather than a home.

The air-conditioning of whole rooms could mean their being closed to the public who would then be obliged to view them either from the outside or by some special arrangement inside the rooms. In either case, the great charm and attraction of being able to walk around in a great house and sense the atmosphere, would be lost. In a private house, however, an owner is able to choose the position of a textile and can regulate the amount of light, the temperature and the humidity. The use of a dimly lit corridor as a place for displaying textile pictures and hangings is worth consideration, as is the use of low-powered artificial light with ultra-violet filters.

TEXTILE COLLECTIONS

A serious collector of textile objects has special problems of display and storage relating to his own particular interest and, if the collection is valuable, there is also the question of security. It is wise to keep a good colour photograph and detailed description of each piece in a safe place away from the collection. For actual display, it might be worthwhile to provide a small, secure area with good, safe conditions as regarding light, temperature and humidity, and show only a few items at a time, varying the display at intervals from a main collection which could remain safe in storage, but easily accessible both for reference and the examination by fellow collectors when required. An index or good labelling system will facilitate easy identification in storage. Providing that the alteration of the display does not entail a great deal of handling, the objects would benefit from less exposure to light and the outside atmosphere and the period of rest that good storage facilities provide.

MOUNTING TEXTILES FOR FRAMING

Smaller and more fragile textiles, for example embroidered pictures, pieces of lace or samplers, are more safely displayed by being mounted behind glass in a frame. The first essential is that the textile should be clean and it is quite possible that it may also require some support or repair before being mounted. How to carry out these processes is explained in later chapters but, for the moment, we will assume that the piece is clean and strong.

In the past, the normal method of mounting a textile for framing seems to have been to attach it with tacks to a wooden stretcher which was like a rough frame, as most people who take an old textile from its frame will find, although occasionally the textile was simply backed with a piece of cardboard. The wood of a stretcher might have warped by changes in humidity causing the wood to shrink or swell and this will have altered the tension on the textile. The tacks holding the fabric to the stretcher often are found to have caused damage by rusting and rotting the fibres or by cutting into them and breaking them. Moreover wood which becomes damp will stain any material with which it comes into contact and this has often been the case if there has been a supporting piece across the stretcher in a rather large fabric picture. Most old frames will be found to have allowed a great deal of dust and damp to enter and the centre of a fabric mounted on a stretcher will almost certainly have become very dusty. In short, experience gained in seeing the long-term effects of this way of framing textiles has prompted us to advocate another method which gives the textile greater all-over support and affords better protection against the damaging effects of damp and dust.

It is not advisable to use cardboard as a mount as this might contain an acid harmful to textiles and is also liable to absorb moisture. More suitable is a piece of hardboard which has been cut to a size very slightly larger than the area of the textile which it is intended to show when in the frame. The hardboard is then covered with a piece of linen or similar material made of natural fibres, cut about three inches larger on all sides than the hardboard. The linen is placed over the smooth surface of the hardboard, absolutely straight, and then stretched taut and fixed by turning the extra three inches on each side over to the rough back of the hardboard and sticking them down with a polyvinyl acetate adhesive, taking care not to allow any of the adhesive to get on to the front or the edges of the hardboard. The corners of the linen should be trimmed so that, when the sticking is done, there is as smooth a finish as possible. It is important that the threads of the linen are straight in both directions and that the linen is stretched taut across the front of the hardboard. The linen-covered hardboard should then be put under weights to give the adhesive twenty-four hours to dry thoroughly before mounting the clean textile.

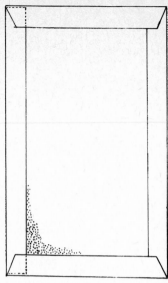

LINEN STUCK TO HARDBOARD AS SEEN FROM BACK

Starting at the top, pin the centred textile to the edge of the linen on the hardboard, making sure that the edge of the textile is as straight as possible. Remember that pins, like needles, should go between threads and never be allowed to split them. Gently pull the textile into position and then pin it to the bottom of the linen-covered hardboard in the same way. Next pin the sides. At all times, be prepared to remove pins and gently pull the textile into place, adjusting until all is straight and even. It may take quite some time to get it quite right, taking pins out, making adjustments, easing or stretching and replacing pins, but, eventually, it should be possible to get all the threads straight and the warp and weft threads of the textile at right angles to each other. Now stitch the textile on to the linen all round the edge, using button thread and an oversewing stitch, removing the pins only after the stitches have taken over the job of keeping everything straight. Mounting a piece in this way can be quite difficult but it is worthwhile to go on adjusting until everything is as straight and pleasing to the eye as possible. A line in a framed piece that is wavy but should be straight can be a continuing source of irritation once the piece is framed and, therefore, time spent in achieving visual acceptability will never be wasted.

Once the textile is mounted, the frame can be made to size. Choose a suitable moulding, if possible one with a deep rebate. It will be necessary to insert a very narrow fillet of wood, mitred at the corners, inside the frame so that the framed textile will never be touching the glass. A picture framer will recognise this as the way that pastels are framed. Whether the fillet is of natural, stained or gilded wood is a matter of choice to suit the textile. It might even be so narrow that it cannot be seen at all. However, if it is visible, its width may be useful to cover up the stitches attaching the textile to the linen-covered hardboard mount

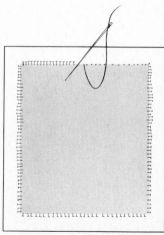

STITCHING TEXTILE ON TO LINEN-COVERED MOUNT

or its colour may serve to enhance the appearance of the textile it surrounds. These decisions are a matter of personal choice, but what is important is that the fillet should be there to prevent the textile from coming into contact with the glass. The glass itself should be sealed into the frame to prevent the entry of dust and damp and this can be done by using narrow strips of a self-adhesive masking called Tuftape which is made by the Copydex firm. Carefully applied, the sealing strip of Tuftape is invisible from the front of the glass. When the glass has been sealed in, it should be throughly cleaned and dried before the fillet is inserted. Perspex Polish No. 3 is an anti-static polish and can be used on the inside of the glass. After the fillet is in position, the hardboard mount, with the textile sewn to it, should be dropped gently into position and kept in place with panel pins or brads. First put one pin in each side of the frame and then turn the frame over to check from the front that all is well and there are no stray pieces of fluff or thread on the picture. Sometimes tapping the brads into place can cause movement and it is as well to check before putting in all the pins. When the hardboard is in place, seal all round the edges of the back of the frame with strips of Tuftape, then cover the whole back of the picture with a sheet of brown paper, sticking it to the hardboard, and finally seal round this backing with brown gummed paper to tidy the edge. Then put in screw eyes to hold the cord for hanging.

Framing lace for display can be done in much the same way, although in this case, the lace would first have to be stitched on to a backing and then the whole attached to the linen-covered hardboard in the manner described above. It pays to experiment with different coloured backgrounds before making a final choice. Although it would seem logical and obvious to choose a contrasting colour in order to show up the pattern of the lace, a more subtle and pleasing effect can often be achieved by choosing a backing of material only slightly darker in colour than the lace itself. Once chosen, stretch the backing on to an embroidery frame and apply the lace to it, using as few, unobtrusive stitches as possible, only just enough to keep it in place.

An alternative to the fillet is to make a sub-frame of balsa wood and

 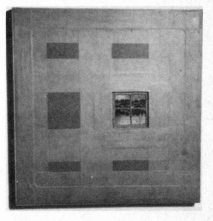

to cover this with the same material as the mount. Apply polyvinyl acetate adhesive to the back surfaces only of the sub-frame to fix on the material so that, although the other faces of the frame are covered with the material, they have no adhesive on them. This is the method which was used in framing the Coptic piece illustrated in the photograph. Remember that, when using a sub-frame of this kind, the rebate of the moulding chosen for the main frame will have to be deep enough to accommodate not only the glass but also the balsa wood sub-frame and the hardboard mount. The type of moulding used in the illustration is known as hockey-stick and the frame was painted to harmonise with the background material. Of additional interest is the window cut in the hardboard backing and covered with Perspex. This allows examination of the Coptic weaving from the reverse side. Stump-work pictures or raised-work embroidery will also need a deep sub-frame to avoid the textile coming in contact with the glass. Fans can be framed in this way, too, although specially made fan cases or box-frames, an example of which is illustrated, would be more suitable.

FAN CASE

When cleaning the glass of either frames or display cases, choose one of two methods. Either use a damp cloth or leather, or use Perspex Polish No. 3. Rubbing glass with a dry cloth can create static electricity and this can draw the fibres of anything behind glass towards the glass and cause strain which, over a period of time, can cause the fibres to break, especially in the case of embroidery. A few drops of an anti-static, such as Comfort or Softrinse, in the water in which a duster or leather is dampened will be an added safeguard. Perspex anti-static polish can be removed by water so, if polish-treated glass is ever washed, the polish will need to be renewed after drying.

TYPES OF DISPLAY AND CARE

Carpets and Rugs

Valuable carpets and rugs, especially those which are walked on or have furniture standing on them, should always be provided with an underfelt of natural fibres and they should be regularly vacuum-cleaned through monofilament screening. If a treasured carpet or rug requires more cleaning or needs conservation, it should be sent to a professional for treatment. There are some first-aid measures which can help to keep carpets and rugs safe and these are dealt with at the end of the chapter on tapestries. The British Museum have published a booklet about clothes moths and carpet beetles which gives valuable information and is well worth reading and keeping for reference.

Hangings

All textile hangings and curtains should be lined, both for their support and to protect them from the dust which always seems to rise and settle on the back of a hanging. In the case of curtains, a lining and interlining will give protection from some of the light they inevitably receive. If curtains are to be drawn across windows, cords should be fitted for this – they should not be pulled by hand.

The choice of lining material is important. Linings should always be lighter in weight than the textile they support – a silk embroidery would require a silk lining and an interlining of suitable material such as bump for protection and to make the piece hang well. If there is any likelihood that the lining material might shrink if it becomes damp, then it should be shrunk before use by being soaked and allowed to dry. Later shrinkage of lining can result in the lining causing damage rather than giving support to the textile.

Allow for the fact that the lining may well be stronger than the textile it is supporting, so be sure that it is attached loosely enough not to exert any drag or pull on the older and probably more fragile textile, and that it also fits well enough to give support. The linings of small hangings need only be attached round the outside edges, but larger textiles should be lined in the same way as curtains. The method of lining a large tapestry is fully described in Chapter Five and can be adapted for lining other textiles. We would recommend the following ways of hanging a lined but unframed textile.

The piece may be suspended from a rigid pole or rod chosen for its suitability both in appearance and strength. For instance, a piece of Oriental embroidery or a Tibetan tanka might look well hung from a piece of bamboo which would be quite strong enough to take the weight, while a piece of tapestry, a rug or heavy fabric collage would require a metal rod to support it as it hangs.

A *sleeve* can be made at the top of the lining through which the pole is put and then the pole itself can be attached to the wall either by hooks at each end or by cords or chains from a central hanging point. The sleeve may be of the same material as the lining, or, if the hanging is heavy, a webbing sleeve would be stronger and more durable. To make the sleeve, cut a strip of material or webbing slightly longer than

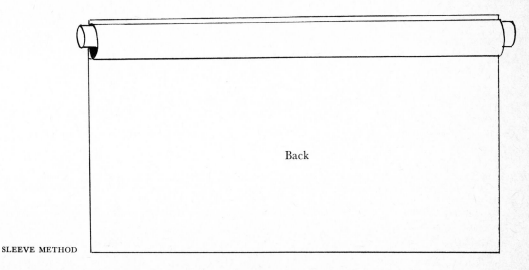

Back

SLEEVE METHOD

the width of the hanging and make a hem at each end, if necessary, turning in the raw edges at top and bottom of the strip. Now stitch the strip in a straight line just below the top edge of the hanging. Place the hanging rod inside the strip and mark the position of the bottom edge of the strip on the lining, remove the rod and stitch the strip along the marked line. The little tunnel thus produced will take the rod and accommodate it in such a way that, when the textile hangs from the rod, it will hang straight down and will not bulge out along the position of the rod.

A rod can also be threaded through tabs of suitable material which have been made above the top edge of the lined textile, as illustrated. This is particularly effective when hanging a textile which has been mounted on to a large piece of material, giving the appearance of a frame. The tabs would then be made of the same material as the mount. Otherwise choose material for the tabs which complement the fabric of the hanging.

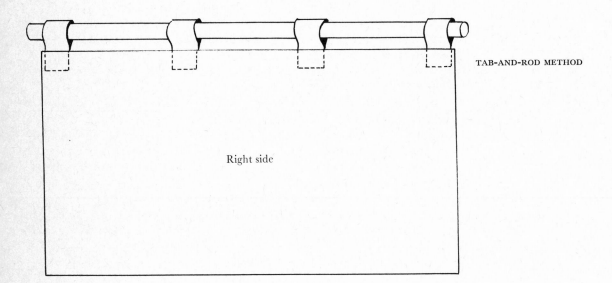

TAB-AND-ROD METHOD

Right side

A very flimsy hanging or one which is rather long and narrow, can be given the weight to hang down straight, provided it is evenly strong and well-supported, by inserting a rod in a sleeve at the bottom as well as at the top of the hanging. Alternatively, weight can be added to the bottom by inserting weighting strips as supplied by haberdashers for use in curtains.

The Velcro method of hanging can be used successfully for small hangings as well as for tapestries, and this method is described in more detail in Chapter Five. A strip of Velcro, the contact fastener, is stitched along the top edge of the lining and the corresponding strip of Velcro is nailed to a batten of wood fixed to the wall where the piece is to hang. By pressing the two strips of Velcro together, the piece will hang safely and well-supported. Only a narrow width of Velcro is needed, and, as in the case of its use on tapestry, the softer of the two strips is sewn to the textile while the stiffer one is nailed, with tacks, to the batten. Part of the charm and character of a textile hanging is its ability to move slightly and one would not wish to lose this by making it too rigid. However, it is not wise to place hangings where they are constantly moved by draughts or where people can brush against them in passing as excessive movement or rubbing will cause damage.

One way of protecting a treasured textile hanging from receiving too much light is to have another attractive, but more expendable, hanging ready to put in front of the valuable one. This is especially sensible if the room is greatly used. There are various ways to fix the protective hanging – it can be put up as a curtain and drawn aside to reveal the older textile behind it, or it could have its own hooks and merely be hung up when required as protection. Be careful that there is sufficient space between the two textiles so that the more valuable one is not rubbed by drawing or fixing the protective hanging in front of it.

Freehanging textiles become dusty and should be cleaned occasionally on front and back with a vacuum-cleaner through nylon monofilament screening. The method for this is described fully in the chapter on cleaning.

Textiles Used in Upholstery

Furniture covered with old and valuable textiles should always be placed so that they do not receive direct light and, as far as is possible, in an atmosphere of constant temperature and humidity. Remember that textiles attached in any way to wood will suffer strain if the wood itself responds to changes in atmospheric conditions by contracting, expanding or warping. If furniture polish is used on the wood, be careful that none is allowed to get on to the textile upholstery as it may stain, it attracts and holds dust and is almost impossible to remove. Silk damask, woven tapestry, embroidered canvas-work and beadwork and velvet are some of the many beautiful textiles which have been used to cover pieces of furniture. A very careful watch should be kept on such textiles, especially if there is any silk in the design of the actual material, or in the embroidery on it, as silk fibres are very vulnerable to the effects of light.

Loose covers can be used as protection but the textiles beneath these covers need to be inspected regularly and the covers themselves kept very clean so that particles of dust and dirt do not work their way through. Loose covers are to be recommended if the furniture is in fairly frequent use. Otherwise, some protection can be given by covering the textiles on furniture with fine net or washed silk crepeline in a suitable colour through which the design should be visible. A net or crepeline cover will not prevent actual deterioration, but will ensure that any potentially loose threads are kept in place and not rubbed away and lost. To fit a net or crepeline cover, smooth it gently over the textile, making sure that all threads are in their proper place and then secure the covering to the underneath of the seat or behind the back with stitching, using a fine curved upholstery needle and silk thread to match the net or crepeline. If the particular design of the furniture makes it impossible to put the protective covering right over the seat or back, then fix it in place by stitching it to the edge of the textile covering, using a curved needle, silk thread and the minimum number of stitches to keep the cover in place. It may be possible to stitch it to the decorative gimp. Valuable cushion covers can be protected in a similar way.

Cleanliness is important and surface cleaning of textiles covering furniture should be done with a vacuum-cleaner through nylon monofilament screening. This is more fully described in the chapter on cleaning.

The less any old and fragile textiles are handled the better, particularly if there are any metallic threads in the design, whether in the weave or as embroidery. Apart from the unnecessary wear and tear, even apparently clean hands can be acid and cause tarnishing by touching. In professional embroidery workrooms, frequent hand-washing is obligatory for those working with metal threads, and there are actually some people whose skin is so acid that, even though their hands seem clean and dry, they are unable to touch gold or silver thread without causing very rapid tarnishing. It requires an effort of will to train oneself, and of tact to restrain one's friends, to resist the temptation to hold, handle and stroke precious pieces, but that restraint is a form of preventive conservation to which everyone can contribute.

Costumes

When as in silk my Julia goes,
Then, then, (methinks) how sweetly flows
That liquefaction of her clothes.

— ROBERT HERRICK, *Upon Julia's Clothes*

If old costumes are collected or owned, their continual safety will be of great importance whether they are on display or stored away to be viewed occasionally and, if one cares for them responsibly, they should never be worn or even tried on. The exceptions here are wedding veils and christening robes when sentimental or traditional reasons for their being worn might outweigh all other considerations. We have dealt with these in more detail later.

If a costume is to be put on display at any time, it should be supported in such a way that no strain is imposed on any part of the fabric. Ideally, one would use dummies made to the exact measurements for each separate costume and would dress the dummies first in the proper undergarments, being especially sure that such intrinsic parts of the costume as, for instance, a bustle are used under the displayed costume, rather than to try to achieve an effect with padding only. Proper underclothing, even petticoats, beneath a costume, not only give the correct appearance but also act as support for the textile of the garment.

SHOULDER SUPPORT

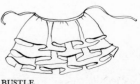

BUSTLE

Crumpled acid-free tissue paper can be added as padding to fill out the costume in such areas as the sleeves. Costumes are always more safely displayed in the round on a dummy, than by using any method which would involve pinning to keep the garment in a display position, say on a board either sloping or vertical, as this causes strain from the points of contact and can, in quite a short time, result in considerable damage.

Any creases in a silk or woollen garment will fall out and disappear if the costume is put on to a dummy or hung up on a well-padded hanger. Ironing should be avoided if at all possible and certainly no textile should be ironed, even at the low temperature (100°C) we recommend, unless it has been cleaned. The heat of an iron can set any stains permanently and any acid dust on the textile could be sealed into the fabric by the application of heat. If a costume is to be shown for any length of time, it should be housed in a display case with a cool, dry atmosphere inside, sealed against the entry of dust and damp and exposed to a minimum of light with an arrangement for complete light exclusion at times when the costume is not on view. Some silica gel crystals in the case will be some protection against damp but the effectiveness of these crystals is limited and they have to be kept under supervision so as to be dried out when they have become saturated.

The temptation to wear and display old and beautiful clothes is great and it can certainly be argued that, as clothes are made to be worn, it is only when they are on living and moving people that the clothes can really be appreciated. This argument has validity but against it can be set the facts that any handling is potentially damaging to an old textile and that great stress and strain is imposed on a costume by dressing and undressing, especially if the wearer is not quite the right size for the garment and is not wearing the underclothing appropriate for the period of the costume. Wearing can also result in staining from perspiration or spilled food or drink. Sitting down in a fragile dress could well ruin it for ever. For a collector determined to display costumes on living models, it would be worthwhile to have copies made for wearing in order that the originals may be kept safe.

There is another way of showing a costume collection safely, again and again, and that is by making a film. People of the right sizes, wearing underclothing appropriate to the costumes, their hair styled correctly and carrying the right accessories, could model the clothes in suitable settings, and all could be recorded on film. Obviously a good deal of planning would have to be done and an undertaking of this kind would be expensive. An added interest would be created if details of the cut, material and stitching of the different costumes were to be shown in close-up. The finished film would be both interesting and educational, much more revealing than a series of photographs and much less dangerous to the costumes than constant wearing and handling.

CHAPTER THREE

Storage

The greatest number of textiles which have survived from very early times are those which have been discovered in tombs, particularly in Egypt and in South America. They could well have been new and of good quality when they were sealed away in what were virtually ideal conditions for the safe keeping of textiles – cool, dry and dark, with a constant temperature and humidity, unpolluted air and, of course, no handling or disturbance.

Their state of preservation provides a good lesson regarding the safe keeping of stored textiles. The opposite is true of airing cupboards, which seem to be unique to Britain. Certainly those airing cupboards built around unlagged hot-water storage tanks have been responsible for damage found in weakened and discoloured fibres along folds and creases, due to pressure, overheating and high humidity. Fortunately, an airing cupboard is not normally considered as storage for treasured textiles, although it is not unknown for some quite old and valued table or bed-linen, not in constant use, to be put there and forgotten until it is too late to prevent damage. The provision of a suitable storage environment is one which must, of course, depend on the facilities available.

SAFE STORAGE

Few, if any, can hope to provide anything approaching the equable climatic conditions afforded by a burial chamber, but everyone trying to supply safe storage for their textiles can do their best in existing or achievable circumstances, using cupboards, shelving to hold boxes, chests of drawers or even special rooms, according to the size and number of the textiles to be stored. The aim should be to provide space that will be dark and dry with a cool, even temperature and sufficient room to accommodate the textiles without overcrowding.

The textiles to be stored should be as clean as possible so that dust and dirt, the acids of atmospheric pollution or the presence of moths or other pests will not cause avoidable deterioration during storage. The method of cleaning textiles is a subject in itself and this is dealt with in a later chapter. A stored textile should not be subjected to any strain or movement which can cause the fibres to become weak and break. Strain can be avoided by seeing that the textiles are supported during storage and are not pressed into sharp folds which will weaken the fibres bent under pressure.

A really good supply of acid-free tissue paper will be needed to protect the textiles. This tissue paper is sold in packets at Woolworths or any stationers. Small, flat textiles, for example pieces of lace or similar items, can be stored lying flat, smooth and unfolded with plenty of acid-free tissue paper above and below each piece. Providing the pieces are not heavy and are quite flat, they can lie on top of each other. Always keep a reference of the position of each item – either with a list on top showing the order or by tabs between each layer – to make identification simple so that each piece is readily accessible without unduly disturbing the other objects. Never use self-adhesive tape nor allow any other adhesive in the form of labels to come into contact with the textiles.

Larger flat pieces which have one side short enough to fit on to a storage shelf or into a drawer and small, long pieces, such as ribbons or strips of embroidery, should be stored rolled, right side outermost and not too tightly, around a cylinder of some sort, again using plenty of acid-free tissue paper so that the textile is protected on each side. The cardboard cylinders from toilet or kitchen paper rolls are useful for narrow pieces. Be sure to cover the cylinder with tissue paper before rolling the textile on to it as some cardboard contains acids harmful to textiles. It is a good idea to assume that all cardboard can harm textiles and to protect these from it with a layer of tissue paper. If a textile can be rolled, it should always be done with the right side outermost; this is especially important if the textile is lined so that the right side of the piece will remain smooth even if the lining becomes creased through the difference in tension caused by rolling the piece round the cylinder. It may seem odd to roll an embroidered piece right side outermost, but it is correct and best for the textile. The right side should, of course, be covered with tissue paper as the rolling proceeds. For larger flat textiles, a length of polythene drainpipe, well covered with tissue paper, makes a good cylinder as it is very light in weight and about the right circumference. Larger cylinders made of cardboard can be obtained from shops selling dress materials or carpets, and these are useful for rolling large textiles. The pieces, once rolled, can be stored in the dark, either on shelves, in drawers or in boxes – again all lined with acid-free tissue paper.

Really large objects, and anything shaped or lined, may have to be folded to fit the storage space available. Any folds necessary should be made very loosely over quite thick rolls of acid-free tissue paper. If the textile is pressed down to give a fold with a sharp edge, the fibres along that fold will be weakened and will eventually break. Stored textiles that have had to be folded should be opened out occasionally and refolded in different places. Particular care should be taken that any folds in stored costumes have rolls of tissue paper inserted under them so that they cannot be pressed down to give a sharp edge. A tag or label to identify each piece will save time in finding an object and prevent any unnecessary disturbance.

COSTUMES

The storing of costumes presents quite complicated problems often requiring individual solutions. Small items can be stored flat. Bonnets and other small, shaped pieces should be filled with crumpled acid-free tissue paper until they assume their correct shapes and they can then be put on to shelves or in boxes, but, of course, never one piece on top of another. Garments may be stored on dummies of the right size and shape, and covered with washed calico or gingham bags, closed at the tops to prevent any dust settling on the garment, but left open at the bottom to allow the air to circulate. The bag must be large enough not to crush the garment in any way. The use of plastic or polythene bags in storage is not recommended. When new, a polythene bag can hold humidity and if anything placed in it is not perfectly clean and dry, the bag will provide ideal conditions for the growth of mildew or similar moulds. Polythene seems to attract dust which lies on its surface and, unfortunately, as polythene gets older, it begins to develop tiny holes through which the dust goes on to the surface of whatever is being covered. Cellophane is a safer cover but has the distinct disadvantage in tearing very easily and, therefore, a fabric cover would seem to be the safest and most durable to use.

Ideally, each costume should be stored on its own dummy made to its proportions. Dressing a dummy for storage is exactly the same as dressing it for display, putting on first the underwear, including bustle, underbodice, etc. as required and using original garments or copies. However, in storage, it is wise to use a great deal of acid-free tissue paper to achieve fullness and shape so that there will be as few folds and creases in the stored garment as possible, and maximum support will be given to the material. Quite a lot of tissue paper will be required even on a specially-made dummy particularly in the sleeves, bodice and around the hips. When storing a costume, stitch several tapes to the inside of the top of the skirt and then pin other ends of the tapes to the dummy, using brass lacepins or safety pins. By making the tapes just short enough, it is possible to let them take some of the weight of the skirt and this will greatly lessen the strain on the fabric of the bodice.

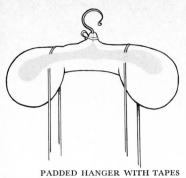

If dummies are not available, costumes can be stored on hangers, very well padded with cotton-wool, and the costume then covered with washed calico or gingham. Never allow a costume to hang from an ordinary unpadded hanger. The photograph illustrates only too clearly what can happen. A very great deal of tissue paper will be needed in the sleeves, bodices and upper parts of the skirts of costumes stored on hangers. Try to make costumes assume, as nearly as possible, their intended shape, eliminating unwanted folds and creases. Tapes again, from the inside tops of the skirts to the hangers, will help to take the strain of the weight of the skirts from the material of the bodices. Calico bags, open at the bottom and closed at the top, should cover the costumes in storage. It is very important to make sure that costumes on hangers are also not packed too closely together, as could well happen if the hangers are put on to a rail in a cupboard. Pushing the costumes together can result in creasing and folding. Here again, we come to the question of space. Tie a label on the top of each calico bag for easy identification of the garment within.

Storing a number of costumes on dummies will take up a great deal of space, as the dummies should not be near enough together that the garments could get crushed. If an open room, rather than a cupboard, is selected as a store, then be sure that the light is excluded and that the temperature and humidity are constant and suitable.

The other possibility for storing costumes is to lay them flat in large boxes, drawers or on shelving. This would be the only sensible way to store a heavily embroidered costume or one with beading on a fragile material, as can be found in some of the dresses from the turn of the century. In such costumes, the weight of the decoration could easily cause damage unless the material of the garment is adequately supported. A dress made of material cut on the cross should always be stored lying flat or it will drop out of shape. Again, a great deal of acid-free tissue paper is needed, with layers below and above each garment and also crumpled into sleeves and bodices so that all folds and creases are eliminated as far as possible and the fabric can rest easily and is well supported. If cardboard boxes are used to store costumes, line the boxes with acid-free tissue paper.

Fans in poor condition which are stored should be loosely open so that there is the least possible strain. Apart from the tissue paper above and below each fan, make up the difference in height between the guards at each side of the fan with rolls of tissue paper to give the fan complete support, and let it lie as flat as possible. Gloves may be stored with folded tissue paper in the fingers and cuffs to suggest their proper shape, and to relax old creases and prevent new ones forming.

Always make sure that anything hard, sharp or rough on the surface of a stored textile, whether it is in the form of a fastening, embroidery, beads or other decoration of any kind, has sufficient padding or protection covering it in storage so that it cannot harm any other textile with which it may come into contact.

The storing of parasols presents a problem. Fully open, the material of the cover is stretched which causes strain, yet if a parasol is stored closed and rolled, the material is again subject to strain from tight folding. If there is sufficient storage room, the covers suffer the least strain if the parasol can be kept just slightly open. Rolls of tissue paper in the loose folds of the cover will ease the material so that the fibres cannot be pressed into sharp folds. Parasols, loosely open, can be supported upright by attaching their handles to a rod across a cupboard, their ferrules just touching the floor, providing they are not allowed to crush or brush against each other. In a later chapter we describe the conservation of a very pretty Victorian parasol and the method evolved to take the strain of tension on the cover of an open parasol by stitching a tape round the inside edge of the cover.

Dolls are best stored individually in boxes, lined with acid-free tissue paper. Lay the doll on a piece of strong clean material which is as long as, and about three times the width of, the doll. Insert rolls of tissue paper under all the potential folds in the doll's clothes to make sure that the material cannot be pressed down into sharp-edged folds. Place a piece of tissue over the whole doll and lift into the box by holding the sides of the material on which the doll lies. Then fold the side pieces of material across the front of the doll. Removal of the doll for examination is then easy, as it can be lifted out of the box supported by the material on which it is lying and need not be handled at all. This method of storage can be adapted for a number of shaped or very fragile objects.

Very lightweight deep frames with fabric bottoms, like the one used for framing the Coptic fragment, can be stacked on top of each other, each one containing some fragile part of a collection. These could even be stored in nicely made containers and lifted out for viewing by means of tapes or tabs.

Examine all textiles, especially stored ones, regularly. There is a preparation called Mystox which is a moth-deterrent, but we believe that constant vigilance is the only sure long-term moth-proofing that there is, providing handling is kept to a minimum. A safety check can, however, be the time to vary the folding pattern in large stored textiles.

CHAPTER FOUR

Cleaning

She did not recognise her enemy,
She thought him Dust,
But what is Dust, save Time's most lethal weapon,
Her faithful ally and our sneaking foe?
— SIR OSBERT SITWELL, *Mrs Southern's Diary*

All textiles should be kept as clean as possible, whether on display or in storage, and, in particular, a textile should be clean before it receives any further treatment of conservation or restoration.

SURFACE CLEANING

Vacuum cleaning, to remove dust, is the easiest form of cleaning for the operator and the least hazardous for the textile, and regular careful surface cleaning is recommended for all textiles on display in open conditions. Hanging textiles need to be cleaned only occasionally, but textiles presenting horizontal surfaces on which dust can collect – for instance, carpets and the upholstery on furniture – require more frequent cleaning. The easiest method to clean the surface of a textile is to cover it with nylon monofilament screening over which the hand-held nozzle of a vacuum cleaner can be quite safely moved to collect the dust. This screening is a very smooth nylon weave, reasonably firm and rigid. It is heavy enough to be laid firmly on the textile so that neither it nor the fibres of the textile underneath are sucked up by the vacuum, although the dust is drawn through it into the nozzle of the cleaner. This screening is also known as filtration fabric. It is sold by length and is about ninety centimetres (thirty-six inches) wide (see 'Stockists' at the end of this book for supplier). For surface cleaning purposes, a piece measuring about a square metre is adequate, as this can be moved around over the whole surface of the textile until it has all been cleaned. As nylon monofilament screening frays very easily, any cut edges should be bound. As it is also very useful as a support for textiles during washing, it is worthwhile to indicate separate pieces used for different purposes by using different coloured bindings, say white for screening used in washing and red for that used in vacuum cleaning, and to remember to keep clean the pieces used with the vacuum cleaner by washing them, separately, from time to time.

If no screening is available, it is possible to clean the surface of a textile by tying a piece of fine net over the hand-held nozzle of a vacuum cleaner and moving this over *and a little above* the textile. This method is not really recommended except in emergencies as great care must be taken so that the nozzle of the cleaner does not touch the surface of the textile being cleaned; this could so easily cause damage by any loose threads on the textile being drawn up by the suction. The use of nylon monofilament screening makes surface cleaning safer for the textile and easier and quicker for the operator.

Brushing, however carefully done, may cause damage and is inefficient in that it tends to move dust around rather than remove it as a vacuum cleaner does. In the cleaning of raised work, dust which has collected in crevices can be gently brushed out with a sable paint-brush so that it can be removed later by the vacuum through screening.

The use of spot cleaners on any textile *in situ* is not recommended, and neither is surface cleaning with a liquid. Any liquid, even plain water, can combine with the chemical content of dust, dirt and the acids of air pollution with damaging effects which may not be immediately apparent but which cannot be rectified afterwards. The cleaning of upholstery while still on furniture, other than the removal of surface dust, should not be attempted.

Any form of chemical dry-cleaning in enclosed premises can be dangerous, not only for the textile but for the operator, too, and should not be attempted. There are specialist dry-cleaning firms which will undertake careful cleaning, giving individual attention to special orders and such firms can be approached to clean dirty but obviously strong textile pieces. It is as well to remember that the decision to have the piece cleaned must ultimately be that of the owner or the person responsible for the care of the textile, and no dry-cleaning firm will accept responsibility for the decision to have the work done. The fluids used in dry-cleaning can cause reactions with the fibres and finishes of some of the old textiles and this may have unfortunate results. Therefore, if the piece is either historically or artistically important, it should be taken to an expert textile conservator for cleaning.

If, however, a piece is not of national importance and, though dirty, is obviously strong, as might be the case with curtains or an item of costume, then dry-cleaning could be done by the owner or person in charge of a piece in one of the coin-operated, do-it-yourself machines with a short cleaning cycle. To prepare the textile for cleaning, first detach anything removable from the textile likely to snag or catch – rings or hooks on a curtain, for instance. If the piece to be cleaned is a garment, remove all non-textile buttons such as metal or horn, do up all hooks and eyes and other fastenings and tack a piece of net or ribbon over them so that they cannot come undone during the movement in the cleaning machine and cause any damage. If there are any other parts of the garment which might be fragile, tack pieces of net over those areas. Make the net patch very much larger than the suspect frail area and take long tacking stitches into the stronger surrounding fabric, using silk thread and a fine needle and fairly loose stitches so that nothing can drag or pull. Also make several rows of long tacking stitches in each direction across the frail area to attach the net and make sure that it will really give support to the potentially weak part. Again, tension is important – stitches should give firmness without being too tight. Now put the prepared textile into a bag made from an old nylon net curtain and sew it up all round before taking it to the dry-cleaning machine.

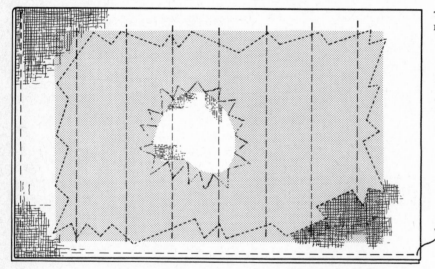

TEXTILE PREPARED FOR
DRY-CLEANING IN NYLON BAG

All this takes time and needs care and may seem excessive pampering of the textile already defined as strong, but prevention of damage is always essential because a complete cure of damage is never possible. After cleaning, hang the textile, on a padded hanger if it is a garment, out in the fresh air to help any creases fall out, and to allow all the fumes from the dry-cleaning fluid to disappear.

WASHING

For many textiles, however, neither surface cleaning with a vacuum cleaner nor dry-cleaning would be suitable or effective and the question arises whether to wash the textile or not. Responsible conservation should use only methods which are reversible – that is, anything that is done can be undone – but washing is an irreversible process and, therefore, the decision to wash is one which should not be made without a great deal of thought, research and tests. Every decision must be a separate one, relating to one particular object only. Experience will obviously be a guide in the decision, but one should never take anything for granted. This is an attitude which it may be difficult for some of us to cultivate since the making, washing and repairing of household linen and clothing is something which, throughout history, has been part of the domestic life, but it does not follow that everyone has been equally skilled in these tasks. Individuals have obviously possessed a greater or lesser degree of competency and when the occasional failure occurred – a colour running in the wash or something that should never have been washed disintegrating in the process – then it was seldom an irretrievable disaster. Clothes and household linens normally wear out and require replacement anyway and an accident or misjudgement could be regarded as merely hastening the inevitable. Successful washing techniques have always needed care, a fact recognised by the many recipes for the safe washing of textiles in books of household management from very early dates. Since the introduction of the more complex man-made fibres which are not always easy to identify, today's fabrics are usually labelled with specific instructions for washing. Some manufacturers, however, still rely on traditional experience by stating simply 'wash as wool'. In the event of a washing failure of a modern fabric, a manufacturer would almost certainly put the blame on the operator for not following the instructions.

Washing an old textile, however, is a very different matter and there can never be any labelled directions. So, first of all there is the problem of identifying the fibre or fibres of the textile, the method of manufacture, the dyes and finishes which have been used and the composition of whatever has made the textile dirty and soiled, including the dust hidden by linings and, sometimes, several interlinings. Secondly, one must assess the condition of the textile, taking into account that all old fibres are almost certainly fragile and that some fibres, even when new and strong, are more vulnerable to damage when they are wet and can more easily tear and break when heavy with water. Finally one must assess the condition and composition of any old repairs, decide if their colours would be fast to washing and, if so, whether to remove them before or after washing. If there is no likelihood of the colour running, old repairs can be some support during the washing process and the decision about whether or not to remove them for aesthetic reasons can be made when the object is clean.

Few textiles with a painted design can be washed. This applies to flags and banners, too, but a fragile flag or banner which has been exposed to atmospheric pollution, whether it has a painted design or not, would have become so acid that putting it into water could be to create a virtual acid bath and result in the disintegration of the textile into a sort of 'banner soup'. The conservation of old flags and banners is professional work. Silk which has been given any form of dressing during its manufacture might never look or feel the same after washing and, therefore no treated silk should be washed. This would apply to most silk garments.

Some dyes can run or bleed if allowed to become wet. Testing by applying wet cotton-wool to an unobtrusive corner of the fabric or embroidery will help to establish if the dyes are relatively fast, but always be wary and careful. The dyes in nineteenth- and early twentieth-century materials, including those used for embroidery silks, are very liable to run. If the dyes appear to be fast but one has some reservations, perhaps because of the date of the object, take the precaution of hastening the drying process after washing by the use of blotting paper or other absorbent material.

If the object to be washed is lined, then always remove the lining and any interlining, and treat the washing of the lining and that of the textile itself as two separate and entirely different problems. The photograph shows what can happen if a lined piece is washed with the lining still in place. The dust and dirt trapped between the lining and the textile have set up chemical reactions which have marked the textile. Unfortunately, even taking the piece apart and rewashing the two textiles separately will not remove such marks, yet it is quite possible that, during the washing and rinsing, all seemed to have been successfully cleaned.

Preparations

Home, and being washing day, dined upon cold meat.

— SAMUEL PEPYS, *Diary*

If a considered decision to wash a textile is taken, then every step of the washing process should be carried out with thought and care. All textiles should be washed lying flat and supported, and handling should be kept to the absolute minimum. First prepare the textile. If it is reasonably strong, then merely laying it flat on a piece of nylon monofilament screening, by which it can be lowered into and raised from the washing vessel, will be protection enough. If the piece is delicate, then sandwich it between two layers of the screening and tack the layers together around the outside so that the textile cannot move around during washing. If the piece is very fragile, then protect the fibres with net in the way described for preparing a piece for dry-cleaning, and then sandwich the textile between two pieces of screening. Try to see that the whole textile is supported and also that there is the least possible chance of the fragile fibres being broken, twisted or pulled out of shape during washing and drying.

TEXTILES USED IN UPHOLSTERY

The textiles to be washed may be covers from pieces of furniture, such as stool tops, chair or sofa seats, backs and armpieces. When a fabric is removed from a piece of furniture for washing, this should be done with great care, not only so that there is no avoidable damage to the old textile covering, but also because the original upholstery materials and methods have their own historical interest and what is found should be recorded in notes and sketches as the pieces are removed. It is always desirable to aim at replacing anything that is in good enough condition, such as the studs which hold the fabric to the wood and the gimp, if it can be cleaned and any necessary repairs effected. On the other hand, of course, this could well be the right time to renew webbing and do any re-upholstery that may have become desirable. If replacements are necessary, try to preserve examples of the original materials to be kept with the documentation on the piece so that all knowledge of the original upholstery materials and methods are not lost. As each textile piece is very carefully removed from the furniture, mark it with a few strands of coloured cotton – a different colour for each piece. Keep a record of where the pieces came from and of the colours marking them. Next make a template, in paper, of each piece, also marking this with the same colour. There should then be no doubt about the size, shape and the exact position on the furniture to which each piece of upholstery material belongs. Prepare for cleaning by supporting fragile areas with screening or net and then, before washing, surface clean each piece on both sides, using a vacuum cleaner and screening, to remove as much loose dust and dirt as possible.

Equipment

Now assemble the equipment needed for washing. The first requirement will be a flat-bottomed vessel large enough to allow the textile to lie completely flat. If one is washing a small item, there is seldom a problem in finding a suitable washing vessel as the kitchen sink, a bowl or bath will do. Especially useful are the shallow tanks used by photographers during developing processes. If the piece to be washed is much larger, it is possible to rig up a washing tank on a terrace or lawn by making an area surrounded by bricks or planks of wood and covering it with a sheet of heavy-duty polythene as illustrated.

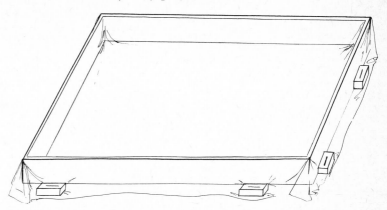

A supply of softened water at a temperature of about 38°C (which feels just warm to the hands) will be needed, on tap if possible. The

49

water we use for washing has first been through a Permutit water softener which has a filter which affects calcium and other minerals. The Permutit needs to be regenerated regularly with common salt. If washing has to be done in water which is known to be hard, both washing and rinsing water can be softened in jugs or other containers by adding Calgon or some other proprietary water softener in the proportions recommended by the manufacturer.

Lissapol N, Vulpex and Saponaria are all suitable as washing agents. Lissapol N should be used in a one per cent solution, adding two 5-ml medicine spoonfuls of Lissapol N liquid to a litre of water (a litre is a pint and three-quarters). Vulpex may be used in a five per cent solution – ten 5-ml spoonfuls to a litre of water – and Saponaria is bought in packets which have instructions on them for preparation. If only a small amount of washing is to be done with Saponaria at any one time, it is wise to make up only a small quantity as it does not keep well once prepared. All these washing agents are mild in action and suitable for washing delicate textiles while almost all the usual washing powders, soaps and detergents on the market contain chemicals and optical bleaches which may make the normal weekly wash 'whiter than white' but which might cause undesirable changes in an old textile, and they should not, therefore, be used in conservation.

A soft flat sponge will be needed for the actual washing; a synthetic sponge will be quite suitable. A quantity of distilled water will also be needed for the final rinses and this should be obtained from a chemist and not from a garage. A piece of soft-board is useful, and sometimes necessary, so that the washed objects can be pinned out to dry, and, as soft-board contains acid, it should always be covered with a sheet of melinex or polythene.

The Washing Process

First make quite sure that everything that will be needed is to hand and prepared, and that the textile is supported adequately and safely.

Having put the warm, softened water and a little of the diluted washing agent into the washing vessel, carefully lower the supported textile into the bath and allow it to become properly saturated. Next press the sponge gently up and down on the textile to move the suds and water through it and release the dust and dirt. Never rub or squeeze an old textile, only press the sponge on it, straight up and down, moving the sponge along as it comes out of the water, so that eventually the whole of the textile has had water and suds pressed through it. If the water becomes dirty very quickly, drain that water away and start afresh. Once the water and the washing agent have done their work and the textile appears clean, let the dirty water drain away and begin to rinse, again using barely warm, softened water – running water if that is possible. If the washing is being done in a sink or bath, and the water is soft, a shampoo attachment is useful here, as it can be held above the textile and moved gradually until the whole surface has been treated, but be sure the rinsing water, too, is only just warm. If washing is being done outside in an improvised washing tank, a hosepipe can be used to carry the water from the domestic supply and the support at one end of the polythene can be taken away so as to allow the rinsing water to drain off the textile. Whatever method of rinsing is used, the water should be softened if at all possible and barely warm and the rinsing process continued until all the suds have gone. The final rinses should be with distilled water. If it is unobtainable, then water which has been boiled and allowed to cool may be used, though boiling only removes a very small amount of the hardness. It is important to finish with the purest possible water. Pinpoints of iron mould on textiles may have been caused originally by traces of iron in washing water, so it is very wise to give a final rinse in pure distilled water, so that there will be the least traces of impurities to leave marks.

The clean textile should be dried flat, right side uppermost, smoothed into shape or, in the case of lace or materials for which templates were made, pinned out into position on a piece of soft-board which has been covered with melinex film, polythene or blotting paper. The pins used should be brass lace pins as soft-board is acid and any other pins can be affected by this. All pieces should be allowed to dry naturally away from bright light, especially sunlight and artificial heat. If there is any suspicion that the colours may run, the drying process may be hastened by the careful use of blotting paper or clean towels. Large pieces, such as a woven tapestry or canvas-work furniture cover, which have been washed in an improvised washing tank outside, should not be left to dry there, even if the day is not especially sunny, but should be blotted with absorbent material to remove some of the water, rolled with more absorbent material round a cylinder, and transported indoors on the cylinder supported by two people, to be unrolled and laid to dry flat, right side uppermost. It will be found that even the largest objects take a surprisingly short time to dry by this method, generally overnight.

LACE PINNED OUT TO DRY

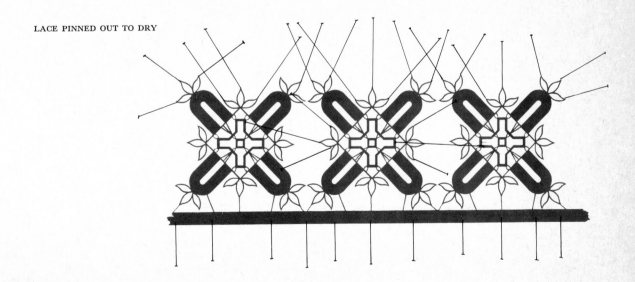

Canvas-work and tapestry furniture covers should be pinned out on melinex-covered soft-board or even on the floor, using the templates to get them to dry into their proper shape and size, with the warp and weft threads aligned at right-angles to each other.

CHRISTENING ROBES

A cotton christening robe should always be washed before storing, especially if the garment has been starched, as starch left in a stored textile can cause damage to the fibres and provide food for pests.

After washing flat, supported on nylon monofilament exactly as described for other textiles, the robe can be dried by being first rolled in a clean white towel to remove some of the water and then hung on a small padded hanger and allowed to dry naturally. It should be gently smoothed and pulled into shape as it dries. When quite dry, it can be stored, using plenty of acid-free tissue paper crumpled into the sleeves and upper part, which may well be embroidered, and with several thicknesses of tissue laid into the skirt of the garment. If possible, the robe should be stored without any folding, but, if folds have to be made, they should be loose ones over rolls of tissue.

When the christening robe is again required for use, it may emerge from storage without needing anything more than an hour or so hanging from a padded hanger to allow any slight creases to fall out, but, if the fabric seems limp, then its appearance will be improved by starching. Use only rice starch (ordinary old-fashioned Robin starch is suitable) but never use any spray-on or plastic starch or stiffener on an old fabric. A very thin solution of starch should be sufficient. Ironing, if needed, should be done with a light-weight iron at the lowest heat setting which will achieve a smooth crisp effect (generally about 100°C).

After the christening, the robe should be washed again, with the greatest care, to remove the starch and any trace of soiling, and the garment returned to storage.

WEDDING VEILS

A wedding veil, like a christening robe, may be a family heirloom which is required for occasional wearing. If the veil has been stored, clean and in good order, either loosely folded over rolls of tissue paper or rolled around a cylinder with plenty of acid-free tissue paper, it should emerge, when required, needing nothing more than shaking out so that it is ready to be worn again. But if it is in need of washing and some repairing, its size makes it rather a problem. The problem, however, is not in the washing but in the space needed for drying. What is needed is a clear space, with a piece of polythene stretched and pinned in place on it, both slightly larger than the veil when it is stretched out to its full size. If those two requirements can be met, the next step is to spread the veil out and examine it carefully for any weak or damaged areas. Extensive repair of a valuable veil should be the work of an expert, but minor tidying up is not too difficult and the veil

can usually be arranged, when it is worn, so that small defects or repairs are hidden in folds. Fine net can be used to patch or strengthen weak areas, using a small embroidery frame as described in the chapter on conservation. Be sure that any patching or tiny darns are made with stitching at exactly the right tension so that there is no pull or drag on surrounding areas. Pay particular attention to the condition of the edges of the veil, if they are fragile or seem likely to tear and break, repair them, either with an edging of fine net or oversewing.

Having made the piece as whole as possible, it will be necessary to reduce it to a manageable size for washing. Spread the veil out again, smooth, flat and in its proper shape, and fold it up for washing. Consulting the accompanying diagram, bring one side edge to the centre (AG to BF), and then the other side edge to the centre to meet the first (CE to BF). Next bring the bottom edge up to the centre (GE to HD) and then the top edge to the centre (AC to HD) and continue in this fashion until the 'parcel' is small enough to fit comfortably into the available washing vessel. When the right size is achieved, tack the square all round using fine mercerised sewing cotton or silk sewing thread and large loose stitches. Now wash the piece, supported on a piece of nylon monofilament screening, in the washing method we have described before. After thorough washing and rinsing, the last rinse in distilled water, keep a little of the distilled water back. Lift the parcel, still on its screening, from the washing vessel, pat with a towel to remove a little of the water, and carry it to the prepared drying area, the clear space covered with the large piece of polythene. Put the wet parcel of veil in the centre of the drying area with its folds facing upwards and cut the threads holding the parcel together. The purpose of the careful folding is now revealed as it is unfolded. It helps to have two people to unfold the veil, one taking each side. Open out each fold and, with care, the veil will come out to its full size without difficulty and without having to be pulled out of shape. Once the veil is opened out completely, wet it all over again with distilled water until it almost floats on the polythene. It will now be possible to pull it all gently and safely into shape. Continue until all is straight and true, paying special attention to the borders especially if these have a pattern of curves or scallops. Pin the veil into position all round the edge, using brass lace pins. Put each in firmly, slanting with the head towards the centre of the veil and then lever it so that it slants away from the veil and produces just a little tension which, if this is the same all over, will ensure that the veil dries in its correct shape and pattern. The veil will dry overnight; make sure that it does so undisturbed. This same method can be used in the washing of lace tablecloths and bedspreads.

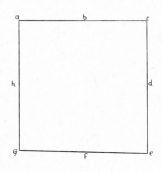

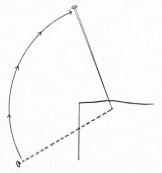

PIN INSERTION FOR DRYING
VEIL IN SHAPE

IRONING

After washing, most pieces, if straightened when wet and allowed to dry in the correct way, should not require ironing. If, however, some ironing is deemed necessary, the temperature of a light-weight iron should not be allowed to rise above 100°C – that is the *cool* or lowest setting on most irons. The application of heat to fibres, particularly in pressing material into sharp folds, is potentially very damaging. If folds are essential to the structure of a textile object – say in the form of pleats – it is better to press these gently into position with the fingers while the fabric is damp and hold them in place on the melinex-covered soft-board with upright brass lace pins, so that the fibres can dry in the required way. Fabrics pleated or folded when first made seem to retain the memory of this and, with a little encouragement, will fall naturally into the desired position.

STAINS

Any stains or spots which remain on old textiles after washing are best left alone, even though there are various commercial preparations available for removing them. This is because the chemicals which these removing agents contain will almost certainly weaken old and fragile fibres, and it is far better to have a spot than a weakened area or even a hole needing repairs which would easily prove more obtrusive than the original mark.

Many bleaching methods are hazardous for old textiles and the result may not be worth the risk involved. All bleaching agents contain chemicals which can harm fibres, as can the old *natural* method of bleaching by drying in sunlight which is also potentially damaging to old fabrics. White lace, in particular, may have acquired a yellow tinge by the time it is old but, providing it is clean, the mellowed effect of age is surely preferable to having lace which has been made white by bleaching but weakened in the process.

To summarise, washing is not only an irreversible process, it is also a potentially destructive one, and the washing of an old textile should be undertaken only after tests, and then using great care. There are many things that can go wrong. Success will be the result of anticipating dangers and taking steps to avoid them, and doing everything carefully and with forethought. Experience will bring confidence but also the realisation that one can never afford to be careless or casual.

CHAPTER FIVE

Tapestries

The arras, rich with horseman, hawk and hound,
Fluttered in the besieging wind's uproar
And the long carpets rose along the dusty floor.
— JOHN KEATS, *Eve of St Agnes*

A tapestry is probably the largest and most valuable single textile that anyone can own, and tapestries are the most numerous of all the really old textiles in this country. Tapestries are very much a part of British history although the number of tapestries actually woven here has been relatively small. Most of the tapestries to be seen now are those covering the walls of castles, great houses and other large buildings, or hanging in museums and art galleries, although there are some still in private ownership. Tapestries are often in series or groups with a common theme, for it was quite customary to buy sets of tapestries with which to line the walls of specific rooms, and generally the subjects they depict are of a heroic nature and scope in keeping with their great size. Favourite subjects were scenes of battle or hunting, illustrations of religious, mythological or allegorical stories, and later ones showed classical or pastoral scenes, often of an idyllic nature with flower-strewn leafy glades and distant vistas of hilltop castles or idealised scenes of country life.

The quality of tapestries varies enormously both in technique of weaving and design. While the weaving of some may be rather loose and coarse, those which were made by later weavers in some of the very famous European workshops are in very fine, close weaving. While many of the early tapestries which have survived were woven almost entirely of wool, weavers working later used much more silk, both for highlights in the actual designs and also for quite large areas of sky.

Metal threads, which had been much used in the Middle Ages and which had probably helped to give the name to the famous 'field of the cloth of gold' of Henry VIII who was well known for his love of and ownership of many tapestries, continued to be used in some of the more opulent tapestries.

Most tapestries are woven on warps of wool, although linen warps were used in some small tapestries. The weaving technique employed is one in which the weft threads are pushed or beaten closely together during weaving so that they cover the warp threads completely, producing a firm fabric. But, by examining a hanging tapestry a little more closely, it can be seen that the warp threads – the strongest and most durable threads in the tapestry which go right through the weaving without a break – are going across the tapestry horizontally, which does not seem right if the tapestry is to be hung for its greatest safety. In fact the tapestry was woven sideways on to the design, a difficult technique even for those incredible craftsmen, the master weavers. Of course there was a reason. The width of any piece of weaving is governed by the width of the loom. Warp threads can be of any length but their number is restricted by just how many can be accommodated side by side in the loom. Anyone who buys material by the metre realises this because cloth is sold in different specified widths depending on the size of the loom on which it was woven, but one can buy almost any length required. One of the original purposes of tapestries was to line the walls of draughty stone castles and palaces, and sets of tapestries which were always very prized were carried around by royalty and noblemen as they moved from one residence to another. Even using the largest available looms, it was not possible to weave tapestries wide enough to cover the high walls and, therefore, their height being that of the width of the loom, they were woven sideways to the required length. This technique has persisted, and has resulted in problems which those caring for tapestries have to solve. The history of tapestries makes fascinating reading and we have included one of the best small books on the subject in the reading list we have given at the end of this book.

ASSESSING THE CONDITION

A hanging tapestry, which does not show any obvious sign of deterioration will hold together, almost from force of habit, for a very long time, providing it is not disturbed. As it is a textile, the effects of light, changes of temperature and humidity, atmospheric pollution and the accumulation of dust are all gradually harming the fibres but, unless it is decided to go ahead with proper conservation in the form of professional cleaning and any other treatment which may be proved necessary, our professional advice would be that it is far better to leave the tapestry alone and not risk damage by disturbing it. Obvious effects of deterioration will occur when any of the fibres become so weak that they finally break and part. This will cause the tapestry gradually to sag in that area and that will put strain on other parts which, if they are also weak, will break and, from this point on, damage will continue at an accelerating rate. The silk threads in a tapestry are more likely to deteriorate and become brittle before the woollen ones except in the case of the dark wool which will have been weakened by its dyeing as in the aforementioned example of the dark outlines in Gothic tapestries.

The washing or extensive restoration of tapestries is professional work but there are certain first-aid measures which can be carefully undertaken by someone who is on the spot, providing that the deterioration is noticed at an early stage. Some of this work can be done while the

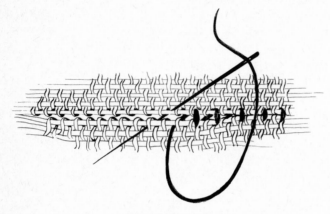

SEWING UP A SLIT

tapestry is still hanging. The weakest parts in the actual weave of a tapestry are the slits which occur where two colours in the design meet. During the weaving, changing from one colour to another was sometimes achieved by twisting the weft threads of the two colours round each other, and this makes the strongest join. Otherwise, one coloured weft thread was taken up to and round a warp thread and then back again, while the other, adjoining, colour was taken up to and round the next warp and back again. This method of changing from one colour to another in the weft makes a slit. When the tapestry weaving was finished, these slits were sewn up, generally with silk. When this silk perishes, and the stitching breaks away, the weight of the tapestry causes the slits to gape open which puts a lot of strain on the rest of the piece. It is possible to sew up gaping slits while the tapestry is still hanging, providing the surrounding areas are in good condition. Use a fine, curved needle and Clark's button thread in an appropriate, unobtrusive colour. It is usual to make the stitches so that they are straight across on the right side and slanting on the wrong side, as we have illustrated. Be very careful not to stitch through a warp thread as this will cause pull and strain. Do not let the stitches catch into the lining. A small pair of pliers is a help in getting the needle through the work. First-aid of this kind, done as preventive conservation as soon as

58

the damage is noticed, will save the tapestry from possible further strain and distortion.

The sky area at the top of a tapestry, especially of tapestries of the seventeenth century and after, was often woven almost entirely with a silk weft. As silk is more liable to early deterioration than wool and is always less strong, this means that, in such tapestries, the weakest area is called upon to take the greatest weight and the condition of that part of the tapestry should always be watched for signs of deterioration. This is not always easy or obvious as the area in question is generally well above eye level. Responsible care of tapestries should, therefore, allow for periodic inspection at close quarters.

If deterioration is detected, then expert advice should be sought. Washing and extensive conservation of tapestries should always be entrusted to a professional. Tapestry conservation is a very time-consuming process, and the more extensive the work required, the greater the cost. Therefore, the earlier the trouble is detected, the less damage will have been caused, and the less time – and therefore money – will have to be spent on treatment. If the expert's assessment is that the tapestry is safe to hang for some time, possibly suggesting that the slits are sewn up and vacuum-cleaning through screening is done, then that advice is reasonably easy to follow, but, if it is necessary to take the tapestry down, then it will have to be decided how and by whom the tapestry is to be removed from the wall.

If a tapestry does show signs of weakness but professional help will have to be deferred and it is important that the tapestry is kept on show, then the tapestry can be taken down and first-aid support can be given to the weak areas by using the lining as a support and stitching the tapestry to the lining in the weak areas. Use Clark's button thread in an unobtrusive colour and take long stitches, being careful not to stitch through a warp thread. The tension of the stitching is important because if they are too loose they serve no purpose, but if they are too tight they will pull and distort the tapestry. This is strictly a short-term, first-aid measure and professional treatment should be given to the tapestry as soon as possible.

TAKING A TAPESTRY DOWN FROM A WALL

Several people will be required to move a tapestry safely from a wall. Even a small one can be surprisingly heavy and no part should be allowed to be without continual support throughout the entire moving operation. Remember, too, that the tapestry will almost certainly be dusty and dirty and could be brittle.

We would never recommend rolling a brittle tapestry sideways off the wall, even if special equipment and manpower were available for this method because, in rolling sideways, the top edge, with its fastenings, becomes increasingly bulky as the size of the roll grows and this, combined with the heavy weight of the tapestry, will inevitably cause sagging which, in turn, will damage brittle silk.

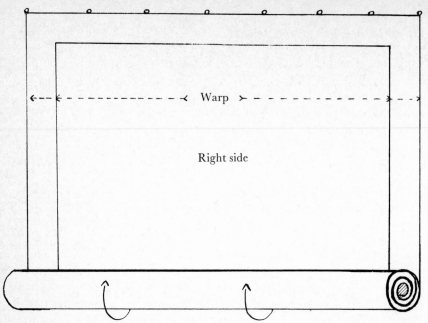

Warp

Right side

A safer way to take a tapestry down is to roll it upwards from the bottom, on to a wooden pole, a cylinder of cardboard or a piece of plastic drainpipe. Whatever is used should be strong enough not to bend or break with the weight of the tapestry and smooth enough not to damage it. It will be necessary to have at least one person at each side of the tapestry to do the rolling up on to the cylinder, with step-ladders to reach the top and, if the tapestry is large and heavy, more people in between to help take the weight. Starting at the bottom, roll the

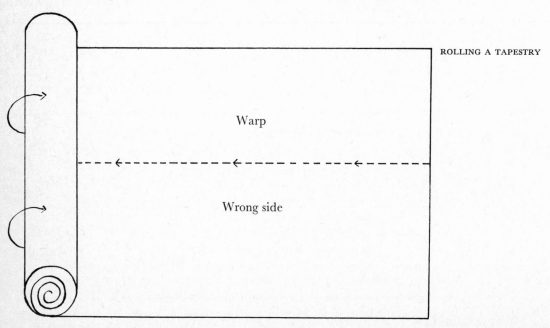

Warp

Wrong side

tapestry carefully up on to the roller until it almost reaches the top where the piece is fixed to the wall. Release whatever is fastening it to the wall and bring the rolled and supported tapestry carefully to the ground. If the tapestry has been attached to the wall by the use of Velcro, releasing it will be very easy; otherwise there may be rings to lift from hooks, poppers to undo or even, although one would deplore this, nails to take out. If the tapestry is hanging on a hoist, letting it down and rolling it on to a cylinder as it reaches the ground will be the easiest way of all. The hoist and Velcro methods of hanging are described later in this chapter as part of the rehanging process after lining a tapestry.

When the rolled tapestry is down, unroll it very carefully on to the floor so that the back of the tapestry is uppermost. If the tapestry is going for immediate further cleaning or conservation treatment, no cleaning need be done at this stage, but, if it is to be stored for any length of time, it is a good idea to clean the back of the tapestry by careful use of a vacuum cleaner through monofilament screening. The next operation is to re-roll the tapestry on to the roller (being sure to cover it with acid-free tissue paper if it is made of cardboard) but this time it should be rolled so that the stronger warp threads go round the roller, in contrast to the way it was rolled when it was taken down, when the weft threads went round the roller. If this is not done, the weft threads are left stretched and damage occurs because old fibres are seldom elastic enough to resume their original length after stretching. To roll the tapestry with the warps round the roller means taking the roller round to the side of the design as in the drawing. In this second rolling, the right side of the tapestry should again be on the outside. If the tapestry is to be stored for any length of time, vacuum the right side as the tapestry is being rolled, again through screening. Once rolled, the tapestry can be covered with a dust sheet and stored lying horizontally on its roller, in a cool, dry, dark place until it is required for rehanging or conservation. A stored and rolled tapestry should always be kept lying down lengthwise so that it is safely supported and the roll should never be allowed to stand upright on one end.

LINING

Tapestries should always be lined, partly because a well-fitted lining provides support and also prevents dust and dirt collecting on the back of the tapestry. Anyone who examines the reverse side of an unlined tapestry will see that there appear to be hundreds of strands of wool and silk hanging there and they will have gathered dust if the tapestry has not been lined previously. If one knows nothing of tapestry weaving, these ends look rather unnecessary and untidy. These are, however, the ends of the weft threads, left by the weavers as part of the weaving process which involved a number of changes of colour and pattern in the design. These weft ends should never be cut off; even their length is critical and they should be left strictly alone. If any of them are shortened or broken off, then the short end will work its way through to the right side of the tapestry and the weaving will gradually come undone.

An examination of the reverse side of a tapestry will also reveal how much the colours on the right side have faded through exposure to light. There was once a quite serious restoration attempt to recapture the original appearance of a faded tapestry by turning it back to front and taking all the loose ends back through the tapestry to the other side, but, apart from the considerable difficulties encountered in that process and the peculiar effect made by all the figures on the tapestry appearing as left-handed, it was then realised that the colours would inevitably fade, and the attempt was not repeated.

Although washing and conservation of tapestries should not be attempted without special knowledge and training, lining a tapestry, while quite an undertaking because of its size, could be done by competent needleworkers, particularly those with experience in the lining of curtains. This work might be a project for a group working in a great house or similar situation. No attempt should be made to line or re-line a tapestry that is not clean and in good condition.

First, decide how much lining is required. Tapestries are best lined with linen or brown holland and this should be shrunk before use (see below), so calculations of the amount required must take into account the loss through shrinking. Supposing the tapestry measures twelve feet by ten feet; the lining, after shrinking, would need to measure at least thirteen feet by eleven feet. If the lining has not been allowed to shrink before it is applied, it could do so afterwards, even by exposure to a damp atmosphere, and this would cause pull and strain on the tapestry. A larger lining would be needed if the tapestry is of a coarse or loose weave because the lining would have to be more loosely applied to make sure that it cannot pull or distort the tapestry.

Work out the amount of lining required, add a generous amount in both length and width for shrinking and buy the linen. Linen sold by the metre is not very wide as a rule, so several widths will have to be joined to make the lining of a large tapestry. These joins should run vertically on the lining.

Shrinking

We find that the easiest way to shrink the linen is to do so while it is still in its uncut length as bought from the shop. Prepare a bath of warm water and lower the length of linen into it in concertina-like folds so that there is, eventually, a folded square of linen lying at the bottom of the bath. Allow this to soak for some hours. The water, which will have probably become quite brown, should be drained away and the linen covered again, this time with hot water. Drain and replenish the water several times more, allowing the linen to soak undisturbed in each lot of water. When the water remains clear, the soaking can stop. Drain the water away and lift the linen on to a pole or board across the bath and let it drip for a while. Then lift it out and undo it on a flat surface, for example a lawn which has been covered with some protective material,

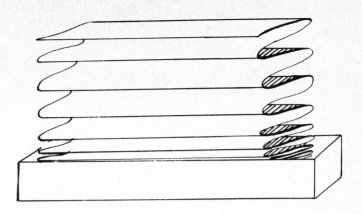

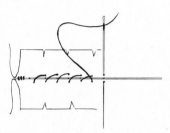

JOINING SELVEDGES OF A LINING

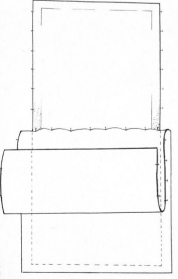

APPLYING LINING TO THE TAPESTRY

smoothing it as flat as possible. When it is almost dry, fold it carefully and put it in a press under a board on which there are as many evenly distributed weights as possible and leave until the linen is quite dry. If the material has been kept smooth throughout the whole operation, no ironing will be needed and, once it is dry, although it will have shrunk, it will be just like material straight from the shop. Ironing is to be avoided because it is almost impossible to iron material without stretching and distorting it.

Next cut the linen into the lengths required for the lining and join these together at the selvedges with machine or hand stitching, making sure that the stitching tension does not produce puckering or strain. When each seam is finished, snip the selvedges every six inches or so and check carefully that there is no puckering along the seams. The seams can be pressed open with the fingers. The lining is now ready to be attached to the tapestry and the method used is very similar to that for curtain lining except that there are more lines of stitching made in attaching tapestry linings in order to provide more support.

Attaching the Lining

Supposing we are still dealing with a tapestry of about twelve feet by ten feet, the clean tapestry should be placed on a flat surface, wrong side uppermost and as straight and smoothly as possible. Ideally, the flat surface should be a table or tables of the same height put together to make the right size. When dealing with a large tapestry, this may not be possible and a clean floor may well provide the only space large enough. For most people, working on the floor is extremely tiring so take this into consideration so that working under these conditions for too long at any one time will not be so likely to result in mistakes due to strain. The corners of handwoven textiles such as tapestries are very seldom a true ninety degrees and, once the piece is laid flat, it may be obvious that it is not a true rectangle or even that the edges are not really quite straight. Put a straight row of pins horizontally across the top edge of the tapestry, just below the edge of the weaving. The actual edge of the textile may waver, but the line of pins should go straight across the top of the tapestry. You can get a straight line the way gardeners do by stretching a cord between two points. Find the exact centre of this line of pins and then make another row of pins at right angles to the top row, going down the centre of the tapestry from the top to the bottom edge. This vertical line of pins may, or may not, be exactly parallel to the edges of the tapestry but should be quite straight and at exact right angles to the top row of pins. Now place the prepared lining on top of the tapestry, right side uppermost, putting the centre top of the lining to the centre top of the tapestry and the centre bottom of the lining to the last pin in the vertical row down the tapestry. Smooth the lining out to make sure that it overlaps the tapestry on each side.

See that there are about two inches of lining above the top of the tapestry and that the lining covers the tapestry completely. Turn the lining back on itself along the central vertical row of pins in a straight line and pin the fold of the lining to the tapestry down the centre line of pins, starting at the top and easing the lining between each pin by pushing it a little towards the top before putting in the next pin so that, although the tapestry still lies quite flat, the lining is very slightly eased as the pins are inserted. A very finely woven tapestry can take a lining that is quite closely fitted but a loosely woven tapestry must have a loosely fitted lining. Once this row of pins is in place, the lining can be stitched to the tapestry, using cotton button thread and a locking stitch which is a loose buttonhole stitch. Each stitch takes up only one warp thread of the tapestry so that it will be covered by the weft. The stitches should be about one and a half inches apart and should finish about four inches from the bottom of the tapestry. Turn the lining back again so that it completely covers the tapestry and again fold it back on itself about thirteen inches from the first fold on the left-hand side of the centre fold. On the tapestry, measure twelve inches from the centre and pin the lining by its fold down a line at this point parallel to the centre, again easing the lining between the pins. The extra one inch of width between the two lines of stitching will also ensure that the lining will not drag or pull the tapestry. Repeat this operation on the left-hand

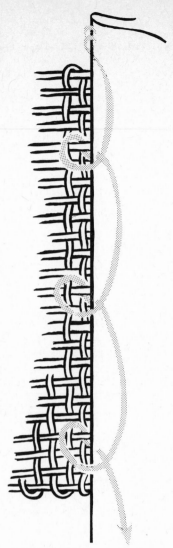

LOCKING STITCH FOR ATTACHING THE LINING VERTICALLY

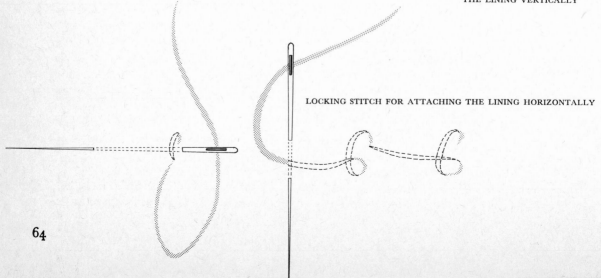

LOCKING STITCH FOR ATTACHING THE LINING HORIZONTALLY

side three times more (five lines of stitching) and then make five similar lines on the right-hand side of the centre line remembering to remove all marking pins, especially those marking the original centre line, before locking on the lining. When the vertical lines of stitching are complete, make horizontal lines, about twelve inches apart, across the lining. These lines are made with stitches catching the lining and a warp thread of the tapestry and then running the needle between the lining and the tapestry for about one and a half inches before coming to the surface of the lining to make another stitch, through the lining and round a warp thread of the tapestry.

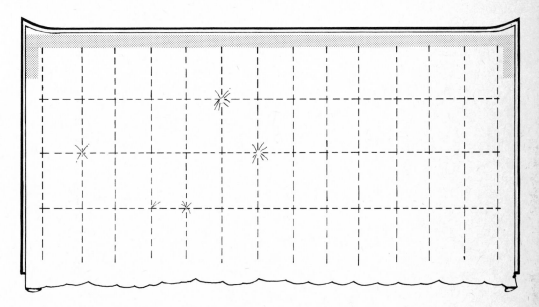

BACK OF TAPESTRY WITH ATTACHED LINING

These vertical and horizontal lines of stitching will give the effect of squares when you look at the lined side of the textile. The sides and top of the lining should be turned under and caught to the edges of the tapestry with slip stitches. Do not, however, sew up the bottom hem of the lining until the lined tapestry has been allowed to hang for a day or two so that it can be seen if there is any drag or pull between lining and tapestry which will have to be relieved and also to let the piece settle and drop if it wishes. After a few days, make any necessary adjustments, turn up the hem of the lining and slip-stitch into place. This method is used for the lining of any hanging textile although, of course, measurements will differ and it may not always be necessary to have so many lines of vertical locking stitches or any horizontal lines at all.

HANGING A TAPESTRY

The best and safest way to hang a textile is by the use of Velcro, the contact fastener. The width of the Velcro chosen should be dictated by

65

the size of the hanging, a strip two inches wide being sufficiently strong even for a heavy tapestry. Making two lines of stitching, one at the top and one at the bottom, sew the strip of Velcro which has the fluffy soft surface to the top of the lined textile, using cotton button thread and a strong needle and sewing firmly through Velcro, lining and textile. A small pair of pliers is a help in pulling the needle through the materials. Fix the corresponding strip of Velcro, which has a rather rough, hard surface, to a wooden batten, using one row of tin tacks along the top edge of the Velcro and one row along the middle, leaving the bottom edge of the Velcro strip free. Now fix the batten to the wall where the textile will hang, remembering to choose a position away from direct light and any source of heat such as a radiator.

By pressing the two strips of Velcro together, the textile will hang evenly supported along its whole width. It can easily be adjusted to hang to the best possible advantage. As already mentioned, the corners of handwoven pieces are seldom true ninety-degree angles nor are the sides always completely straight, and, when hanging a large handwoven textile in other ways, such as with rings along the top or by using a sleeve and a rod, it is often quite difficult to get the piece to hang straight enough to be visually acceptable; the Velcro method makes adjustment easy. A small, but important point, too, is that the hanging can easily be removed for cleaning or in an emergency such as a fire. If the hanging is really very large and heavy, it may be advisable to put additional strips of Velcro, and corresponding battens, at right angles

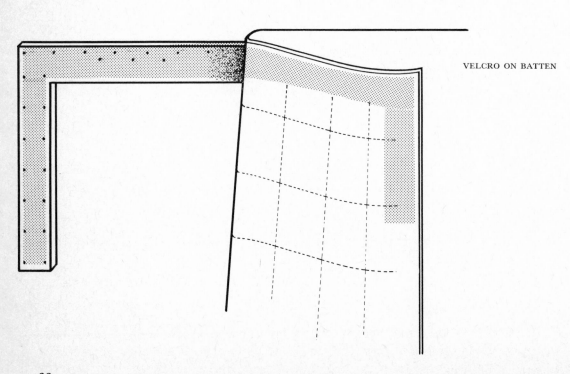

VELCRO ON BATTEN

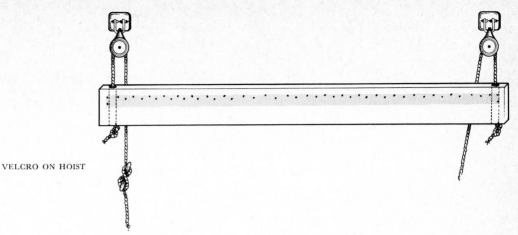

VELCRO ON HOIST

down each of the sides for about two feet from the top for greater support. If it is known that the help available to hang or take down a tapestry will always be limited, or if it is anticipated that the tapestries on display may often be changed around, it would be worthwhile to install a hoist system. This would mean that, instead of nailing the Velcro to a batten fixed on the wall, it would be put on to a length of wood which could be raised and lowered by a simple system of pulleys. Thus, the tapestry could be attached or detached while the cylinder on which it is rolled is still on the ground, and raised or lowered safely and easily.

VACUUM-CLEANING

It is possible to clean the surface of a hanging tapestry, which is in good condition, by using a vacuum cleaner and nylon monofilament screening. The screening can be used in lengths, held either vertically or horizontally and moved along, as each area of the hanging is cleaned by passing the nozzle of the vacuum cleaner over it. If numbers of tapestries are to be cleaned in this way, it would be worthwhile to attach the screening to smooth wooden battens to give rigidity so that the screening could be more easily moved along. Several people may be needed – to hold the screening in position, to hold the cleaner, to direct the nozzle which should be fitted to the longest reaching attachment of the cleaner – and, in the case of a really large tapestry, step ladders would have to be used to reach the top of the hanging. Care is needed at all stages, but this cleaning need not be done too frequently and then should only be attempted on tapestries in good condition which the removal of surface dust and dirt would help to maintain.

CARPETS AND RUGS

Some carpets and rugs with a flat surface may have been woven in almost exactly the same way as a tapestry. First-aid in sewing up slits in the weaving would, therefore, be applicable and the method is the same as that used on tapestries. Worn or fragile areas should be strengthened by applying patches of linen to the wrong side of the carpet or rug with careful stitching, using button thread in an unobtrusive colour and taking care always to stitch between, and not through, warp threads.

The edges of carpets are frequently the first parts to show signs of wear and these can be strengthened by oversewing. Study the way the edges have been finished originally and try to copy this, being careful not to stitch too closely or too tightly because this will only cause strain and damage. Fringes on carpets or rugs are usually the ends of warp threads, possibly knotted or woven with a special finishing border. The fringes become worn and, if this deterioration is allowed to continue, will eventually result in the unravelling of the weaving. If tape or webbing is stitched along the edge on the wrong side, this will give support and the piece will stay safe for a longer period. The edges of pile carpets and rugs can also benefit from similar attention. Never use any adhesive tape or binding on valuable old carpets or rugs.

CHAPTER SIX

Conservation and Restoration

But what is past my help, is past my care.
— BEAUMONT AND FLETCHER, *The Double Marriage*

As every old textile presents its own unique conservation problems, rules for treatment are almost impossible to formulate beyond agreeing that most old textiles will require cleaning and, after that, many will also need some support and, if they are to be displayed, will need to be made as attractive as possible.

We have tried to show in a previous chapter that washing and cleaning old textiles requires a different approach from that normally used for domestic fabrics. Similarly, the techniques used in the conservation and restoration of old textiles are different from those used in mending everyday materials and making-up or embroidering new fabrics. The expert needleworker may find that he or she has to learn to resist the temptation to do too much sewing when trying to save an old textile, and would, in fact, be well advised to regard textile conservation as a skill requiring the adoption of a completely new technique and outlook. Successful treatment is achieved by doing just enough to make an object safe for display, storage or re-use and to make it appear whole and to look right. Although, as with washing and cleaning, it is wise to send any textile which has artistic or historic importance to a professional for treatment, the appearance and safety of many other treasured textiles can, with care, be improved.

Conservation requires that everything that is original on an object be retained and nothing added. Restoration, on the other hand, implies a degree of repair so that the piece not only looks as nearly like it did originally, but it may even be made strong enough for further use. One would conserve a piece for display as part of a collection, as was the case with the piece of Coptic weaving illustrated earlier, but one would restore the old canvas-work or tapestry cover of a chair which is intended for use again.

ATTACHING THE TEXTILE TO A SUPPORT

The most effective support one can give an old and fragile textile is to back it with a suitable material, and choosing the type of backing is of great importance. It should be compatible with the textile it will support and suitable in weight, weave, colour and type of fibre. Again, there are no rules to govern the choice of supporting materials except to acknowledge that natural materials have an affinity for each other, as have man-made fibres.

The way to apply an old textile to its support is by first mounting the supporting material in an embroidery frame. In fact the use of an embroidery frame is almost essential in textile conservation because the tension can be kept constant, handling reduced to a minimum and the work left safely, covered up between sessions of work. The latter is important since textile conservation is something which cannot be hurried; some jobs can take a very long time to complete and this must be accepted.

The type of embroidery frame which is the most useful to have is that which is known in Britain as a tapestry frame (see illustration, page 93). These can be bought in different sizes measured by the length of the tapes or webbing on the rollers to which the material is stitched. A small frame with webbing of eighteen inches in length will take material up to sixteen inches wide but a really large one such as is used in the conservation of tapestries can be over twenty feet wide. Ideally, for each job, one would choose a frame of the right size from a large stock, but they are expensive to buy and if only one is to be acquired then it is always better to have the largest that one can afford or has room to use because, although it is possible to use a large frame for a narrow piece of material, the reverse will never be the case. A frame with a tape size of forty inches will be large enough to take the supporting material for, say, a canvas-work or tapestry sofa back. It will be found useful to have at least one small frame permanently fitted with a piece of linen with the centre missing, as in the illustration. This can be an old picture frame or stretcher with the linen attached and its purpose is to provide a frame for small repairs. It can be put under the area to be treated, the textile pinned or sewn to the linen surround and the frame then raised from the table by blocks or put across a gap of some other kind so that the necessary stitching can be done through the open centre of the linen. This kind of frame can easily be moved around to treat small areas which do not require the backing of a supporting fabric.

To frame up a supporting material in a larger frame, first see that the centre of each of the strips of webbing or tape on the rollers of the frame

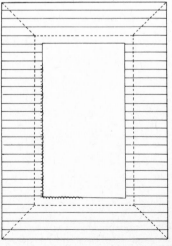

LINEN-COVERED STRETCHER FRAME

is marked. These central marks should be accurate and permanent. Turn the raw edge of the supporting material over about half an inch. This fold should be made on the exact straight of the material. Mark the centre of the fold and pin this to the centre of the webbing on the roller. Bring the folded edge of the material to the edge of the webbing and, starting from the centre, oversew them together. When one half is sewn, start at the centre again and oversew the other half. Roll any material surplus to immediate requirement round one roller. Now attach the other end of the material to the webbing on the other roller in exactly the same way. Put the side pieces into the slots at the ends of each roller and stretch the material out in the frame, inserting the pegs at the sides to keep the material under tension. Make sure that the distance between the top and bottom pegs on each side is exactly the same. The material can be stretched out evenly by putting tapes round the stretchers at the sides and attaching these to the material in the frame. This can be clearly seen in the picture, later in this chapter, of the frame used in the work of conservation of Prince Rupert's coat. These side tapes help to keep the tension even all over the supporting material in the frame.

The tension of fabrics under treatment is very important in the work of textile conservation and can vary for different needs. For instance, when a small piece of old fabric is being supported, the tension of the old and the supporting material should be the same, neither one pulling the other, and this is comparatively easy to regulate. But, when one is dealing with a much larger piece, as would be the case when restoring a piece of upholstery material, there can be difficulties in maintaining the relative tensions; we deal with that problem later.

The correct tension of stitching in conservation is of the greatest importance, too. If the stitches are too tight, they may cut into the old fabric and cause damage, even more so if they are also too small. If stitches are too loose, they will not only be ineffective but will also allow movement between the support and the old textile. Most people tend at first to stitch too tightly, but beware of over-compensating. The ability to judge correct tension in stitching comes with experience, and most naturally and quickly to those with a feeling for textiles. Having the work in a frame makes it much easier to get correct tension.

TREATMENT

What's amiss, I'll strive to mend
And endure what can't be mended.

— ISAAK WATTS, *Good Resolutions*

The actual treatment each object should receive must be decided upon according to its condition and intended future. We have, therefore, chosen to describe the treatment of several different objects or groups of objects, and hope in this way to give as wide a view as possible of what can be done.

Victorian Pincushion Cover

The conservation of what was believed to have been a very pretty pincushion cover said to have been made for Queen Victoria, the photograph of which we chose for our frontispiece, provides an example of saving an historic piece for show while only hinting at its original purpose.

The cover came to us as two separate pieces, a central circle and a surrounding but detached frill. The material was of fine white muslin embroidered with white cotton. The pieces were in fair condition but dirty. Both were carefully supported on net and washed and dried in shape. The very few repairs necessary were done by fine darning, and the frill stitched on to the centre.

A mount was prepared by covering a piece of hardboard with Thai silk in a bluish-grey colour. A circular area in the centre of the mount, the size of the circle of embroidery, was lightly padded with tailor's wadding and covered with a rondel of the same blue-grey Thai silk to give the suggestion of the shape of a pin-cushion. The clean, repaired and reassembled embroidered cover was placed over this raised area and lightly secured around the circular mount with stitching. A few more stitches secured the frill to the mount at intervals round the edge. The mounted cover was then put into a glazed box frame for display.

Piece of Coptic Weaving

The conservation of the piece of Coptic weaving illustrated earlier comes next. Part of the weaving technique used in making this object is similar to that used when making towelling and, after washing, as the piece dried each loop was carefully pulled out so that all the loops dried straight and separate from each other. When the piece was quite dry, it was applied to a piece of coarse linen which had been stretched in an embroidery frame to an even tension. First, the piece was pinned in place with entomological pins, making sure that the warp and weft threads of both the Coptic weaving and the linen were straight. Entomological pins are long and very fine and are invaluable for holding down fragile pieces and loose threads before stitching, being so thin that they can be inserted between the threads of even delicate materials, leaving no hole at all when they are withdrawn.

Once the Coptic piece was pinned in place, a reel of Clark's button thread was chosen in a colour as near that of the supporting material as possible, and a short length cut off for use. This cable-twisted thread will unwind into three separate strands and each of these three strands will, in turn, unwind into three threads, making nine fine threads in all, so that button thread is actually nine fine threads, cable-twisted together. Using a very fine needle and one thickness (one-ninth of the button thread), the Coptic piece was sewn to the supporting material all round the edge and round the missing areas. Stitches were also made to fasten down the loose and damaged threads. Once this was done, the linen supporting the old textile was taken from the frame, cut into a square and hemmed around. In this way, the Coptic piece was given the appearance of being a whole and recognisable shape, missing areas were less obvious and its fragile fibres were supported by the strong linen.

The linen square was then mounted on to another larger piece of linen which had been stretched across the linen-covered balsa wood subframe. This second piece of linen was different in colour, weave and texture but sympathetic to and enhancing the Coptic piece. A small square was cut out of both pieces of supporting linen, and a Perspex-covered 'window' was made in the hardboard backing to reveal a portion of the reverse side of the Coptic weaving which was of special interest. Finally, the whole was glazed and framed in the way we have already described. Nothing was added to the Coptic piece itself, nothing was taken away, but, by putting the piece on to the linen, missing areas appeared filled up and this made the piece look whole and pleasant.

Prince Rupert's Coat

The next example of conservation technique concerns a garment. This was a coat, reputed to have been worn by Prince Rupert of the Rhine. When this beautiful parchment-coloured coat arrived for treatment it was, almost literally, in shreds. The material was woven with a silk warp and woollen weft. The silk warps had disintegrated to a very great extent, as can be seen in the photograph. Obviously the material would need support but this would mean getting it flat, in order to apply it to a supporting material in an embroidery frame. But material which has been made into a garment has been cut and shaped and joined so that few parts of it remain quite flat. It would seem necessary, then, to undo seams to make the various parts of a garment flat enough for treatment. Here we come to another decision regarding the ethics of conservation: the original stitching and making up of an historic garment have a great deal of importance to those who study costume, and it is always desirable to avoid unpicking. In the case of Prince Rupert's coat, it was necessary to apply parts of the coat to the supporting fabric and, fortunately, this was made possible simply by undoing the lining and the seams where the sleeves were set into the shoulders.

The material chosen for support was of man-made fibre in the identical colour of the coat and slightly lighter in weight and very strong.

Polyester fabrics can be very useful as supporting materials, because they are stable and have good resistance to light and humidity. Another possible supporting material would have been silk crepeline but, in this case, it was felt that it would not have been strong enough to give adequate support, nor heavy enough to give back the original weight to the whole garment which had been lost through disintegration of the silk warp.

Having chosen the supporting material, this was stretched into an embroidery frame and the various parts of the coat were laid on it in turn and applied to it by stitching, using a very fine needle and threads drawn from another piece of the supporting material. How this attaching was done is shown in the photograph. The broken threads of the silk were held in place with entomological pins and then stitched down using a pattern of couching – laying fine threads of the man-made fibre across the broken silk threads in long stitches, caught down by smaller stitches at regular intervals. The fine threads of the couching were invisible from even a short distance and the general improvement made by tidying the broken threads of the old material made the piece look whole again. The beautiful parchment lace decoration was vacuum-cleaned and the garment reassembled.

One of the most important results of conserving textiles by stitching is that they still retain their essential qualities of moving and draping after treatment. This method of conservation can be successfully used on almost any fabric and is very suitable for brocade and damask, especially if the colours of the couching threads follow the colours of the pattern on the old material and are fine and unobtrusive. The supporting material must be chosen carefully, both for colour and weight so that, if there are any actual holes or missing areas in the old textile, the supporting fabric shows through and takes over to fill the gap. The casual observer is likely to accept the piece as being in a much better condition than it really is but, for the student who goes near to examine

the piece really closely, the conservation technique is soon revealed, and he can concentrate on his studies of the original textile. The conservation of Prince Rupert's coat was the work of an experienced professional conservator and took about 500 hours, but the technique could be used by less experienced conservators.

Very fine, thin, fragile textiles can be given support by applying them to fine net or silk crepeline. Crepeline should always be washed before being used as a supporting material, to remove the dressing used in its manufacture which gives it body. The method of treatment is much the same as that used in the conservation of Prince Rupert's coat. The supporting material is framed up and the old textile laid on it and stitched with an appropriate thread wherever it needs support. When the pieces are removed from the frame, the net or crepeline can be cut away from the back of the old textile wherever it is not needed.

Doge's Parasol

A rather similar method of supporting an old and fragile fabric using a stitching technique on to a supportive material was employed in the conservation of a beautiful and unusual parasol, said to have belonged to a Venetian doge at the end of the seventeenth century, and now at Waddesdon Manor, Buckinghamshire, which belongs to the National

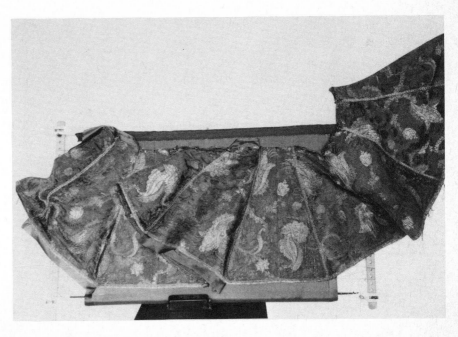

Trust. The outer cover was of red silk brocaded in gold, and the lining was of fine grey-green taffeta which had probably been light blue when new, on which were painted gold stars. The cover, made up of ten triangular pieces, had been removed from the parasol frame in four pieces and washed before it came to us. Unfortunately, no record had been kept as to where each piece went, which made eventual reassembly

very difficult, and proved – if proof were needed – the wisdom of templates and marking and making copious notes whenever anything is taken apart, even if all the pieces appear to be interchangeable, as these did. They were, in fact, all slightly different, but had to go back in the right order, which was very difficult to determine.

The four pieces were supported on nylon monofilament and rewashed to straighten out the weft threads of the brocade which had become rather twisted. When dry, the panels were stitched, section by section, to a support of red jap silk which was mounted in an embroidery frame. The gold braid outline of the gold brocade design was sewn down with polyester threads. Where the warp threads in the brocade were missing,

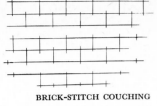

BRICK-STITCH COUCHING

couching threads of polyester were laid and sewn down. The stitches were made over two laid threads in a brick-stitch fashion which broke up the shiny surface of the exposed weft threads, and did not pull them down, thus avoiding that quilted look which can occur when traditional couching methods are used. The silk lining was supported with resin-coated net and the top re-lined with white/cream jap silk as the original lining had disintegrated round the edges where it was fixed to the frame. The gold fringe was straightened and cleaned. The re-assembly of the parasol was difficult, as we said before, because there were no notes or guide-lines and each piece was of a slightly different size.

Victorian Parasol

We treated another parasol – this time a very pretty Victorian one belonging to the Exeter Museum – and in doing so evolved a method of preventing strain on parasols which have to remain open for any length of time as would be the case if they were ever on exhibition. This one was pagoda-shaped, had eight whalebone spokes and a cover of pale green and yellow warp-printed taffeta with a yellow frill, all covered in black silk lace, and a long silk fringe round the edge. The lining of the parasol was of white silk which had been subjected to such strain, owing to the shape of the parasol, that it had split. The parasol was taken apart and cleaned and the damaged lining repaired and strengthened, and then the parasol was reassembled. It was the lining which gave the pagoda shape to the parasol and it seemed sensible to think of a method to relieve the very obvious strain on the lining panels so that they would not split again. The solution to the problem was found by fitting a narrow tape, stitching it to the end of each spoke so that it stretched all round the inside perimeter of the parasol. It was slightly tighter than the outside edge of the lining, and could, therefore, take the strain. The drawing illustrates the position of the tape which is very unobtrusive but, if it is noticed, its purpose is so obvious that attention does not linger on it.

Quaker-dressed Doll

The conservation of items of costume includes, of course, treatment of dolls and their clothing. Undressing an old doll should be done with care and notes should be taken of the order and way in which the clothes were put on the doll. Those who study the history of costume are always interested in clues which will help determine exactly how garments were worn and sometimes a doll may have been dressed in such a way as to help solve some of the puzzles which still remain.

One of the most interesting tasks we had in this area was the conservation of a doll dressed as a Quaker. It was difficult to date the doll exactly because, as a Quaker, one would not expect her to be dressed in the latest fashion of her time, but she was probably dressed at about the end of the eighteenth or beginning of the nineteenth century. All her clothes were dirty and worn but she had a wardrobe of several shawls, both muslin and silk, and two bonnets. All the white fabrics of the clothing could be washed. The white linen apron was very fragile indeed and needed the support of nylon net for washing. All the pieces washed successfully and dried straight and smooth and so did not require ironing.

The skirt of the doll's dress was of silk woven in a plain weave which originally would have made a fairly stiff fabric. Examination of a selvedge inside one seam showed which were warp and which weft threads and we could see that the warp threads were less strong than the weft as the broken parts in the silk all lay in the same direction. It is possible that these warp threads had been given some treatment or dressing before weaving to prevent the silk fraying in the loom and it was this which had eventually weakened the threads. When damage of this kind appears anywhere in a textile, it indicates the possibility that the rest of those threads (in this case, the warps) will be weak everywhere even though they have not yet broken in other areas, and therefore all-over support is needed. After consideration the material of the skirt was detached so that it could be repaired by being supported on a fine polyester crepeline mounted in an embroidery frame and the broken silk was held in place by stitching with a fine silk thread dyed to match. The technique of support was very similar to that used for Prince Rupert's coat.

The bodice of the dress presented greater difficulties. Original stitching used in the making up of garments should be retained wherever possible but as the bodice of this doll's dress was lined, it would have had to be taken apart if it were to be treated in the same way as the material of the skirt. Although repairing through lining is not usually to be recommended because it can make the fabric stiffer and clumsier than it ought to be, it was decided, in this case, because of the small size of the bodice and the importance of retaining the original stitching, that the lining should be used as the supporting material and this was done and no unpicking undertaken.

The doll had only one shoe, made from black satin-woven silk over white alum-treated leather. She wore white gloves, also of alum-treated leather, and these were not removed as they were too brittle and the only cleaning attempted on the shoe and gloves was a gentle dusting with a sable brush. Water would have removed the alum treatment had they been washed and that would have left just old untreated skin. Cleaning fluids would have made the leather more brittle. The missing shoe was replaced with one made up from black felt, simply for appearance's sake. Most of the other items of clothing were in fair condition and were replaced after cleaning.

Two Altar Frontals

An altar frontal dated about 1910 was sent to us for conservation. It was of silk damask with silk and jap gold embroidery. There was considerable damage, from rubbing, to the top of the frontal and some of the silk damask had worn right through. The frontal was first vacuum-cleaned through screening and then taken apart. There had been some previous repairing done by stitching through to the material backing the embroidery and some of these repairing stitches were removed. When the piece was apart, it could be seen that some extra

of the original damask had been folded back round the edges when the piece had been made up, and that the embroidery had been correctly done through the damask supported by a backing material. The damask and supporting material, now as one, were put into an embroidery frame, and pieces of this extra damask were cut off and put between the damaged damask and the backing, in such a way that the pattern of the damask was matched in these patches. The pieces were held in position with a couching method of stitching and the repairs effected so that the top of the damask looked whole again. When all the damaged areas had been treated, the frontal was reassembled.

The second altar frontal had very heavy gold embroidery on a thin silk fabric, but this work had been done without the support of a backing material. When new, the frontal must have looked very lovely and must have been the result of a great many hours of work but, because the background material was very thin and had been called upon to take the considerable weight of the gold embroidery, it had disintegrated to the point where it could no longer give support. Transferring as much as possible of the original embroidery to a new material, suitably backed with a firm linen support, and replacing that part of the embroidered design which it was impossible to transfer, would have been the only way to save even part of the frontal and this would have been a very lengthy process, expensive beyond the value of the piece. Weighty embroidery, particularly if metal threads are used, should be really well supported not only by the materials on which the work is done, but also with an adequate backing to that material. Had this frontal been properly supported by a backing in the first place, even the rather thin material chosen would have survived much longer than it did.

An Incomplete Costume

To make an object comprehensible in display, it might be necessary to add the semblance of a missing part. We can quote the case of the nineteenth-century dress acquired by a collector and brought for treatment. The dress material had come from India and was decorated with a design made up of beetle-wings. These green, iridescent, sequin-like wings gave a most unusual and attractive appearance to the material. The dress, unfortunately, had no sleeves and meant very little to anyone in its incomplete state.

Research was done to find what sort of sleeves a dress of that style and date could have had, and a possible sleeve pattern was established. New sleeves were then made, using a modern fabric as nearly matching the original material of the dress as possible. Our collection of potentially useful items yielded just enough similar beetle-wings to decorate the edges of the new sleeves. To the casual observer, the dress would seem to be an authentic example of its period. A serious student of costume, however, while agreeing or possibly disagreeing with the style

of the new sleeves for the dress, would see at once on closer examination that they were not original. The addition of the new sleeves made the dress understandable for display but no attempt had been made to deceive. The material of the main part of the dress provided a good example of the method of using beetle-wings as a decoration and, as such, deserved to be seen.

TAPESTRY AND CANVAS-WORK

Woven tapestry is often used as an upholstery material and may need restoration so that it can continue to be used. Even more common is the canvas-work embroidery which is frequently called tapestry. This description has almost become accepted as correct in Britain, where noblewomen were never associated with weaving on a loom as they were in some other parts of the world, such as Germany and Scandinavia. From Tudor times, British needleworkers have imitated woven tapestries by embroidering on canvas, and their work has become known as tapestry work or, simply, tapestry. In America it is called needle-point, possibly because *gros-point* and *petit-point* are the two most commonly used canvas-work stitches.

It is essential to know the difference between tapestry and canvas-work, and how each was produced, if one is going to do any conservation or restoration on either of them. Tapestry has been woven on a loom using a plain weave in which the warp threads are closely covered by the weft threads. Canvas-work, on the other hand, is embroidery done with a needle and threads of wool or silk on an existing base of canvas.

The replacement of missing stitches in canvas-work or the restoration of fragile areas in woven tapestry, should always be done on to a supporting fabric. We use linen scrim, the material used for cleaning windows, as a supporting material for canvas-work, and for tapestry we use scrim, linen crash or brown holland, which is also used for linings. These materials need to be allowed to shrink before use, so that there will be no danger of their shrinking later which could cause strain and pull on the textile they are supporting. Our method of shrinking has already been described in the chapter on tapestry. If the material is kept smooth throughout the process, no ironing will be needed. The amount of shrinkage will vary but 'before' and 'after' measurements will always prove the wisdom of shrinking before use as, otherwise, a damp atmosphere could cause problems later.

The next stage is to frame up the supporting material. The frame must be large enough to take a piece of linen or scrim which will allow a border of at least two inches all round the textile to be treated. The upholsterer will be glad of this border to pull on when returning the restored textile cover to its piece of furniture. Sew the ends of the linen or scrim firmly to the webbing on the frame rollers and roll the material evenly up from one end until there is a reasonable area on which to work. Put stretchers into the sides of the frame giving the framed support material an even but slightly slack tension. As stitching is done through both the supporting and the old textile, the respective tensions are important. The old textile should be comfortably stretched and taut during treatment but, if the supporting material is too tight, it will pull and distort the old textile. On the other hand, if it is too loose, it will not give adequate support. If despite all your care, there should be a tight area, once restoration of the piece is finished and it is removed from the frame, it is possible to relieve the tension by slitting the supporting fabric where no stitches come through. Quite a small slit will make a great difference.

Once the supporting material is in the frame correctly, first pin and then, using button thread, stitch the bottom edge of the old textile to it at one end about three inches up from the webbing. If the piece to be treated is canvas-work, place it so that the design is right way round and work from the bottom upwards. If the piece is tapestry, however, it is essential to see that the warp threads run from the bottom to the top of the frame, parallel with the side stretchers.

After having secured the bottom edge of the piece to the supporting material in the frame, pull the tapestry or canvas-work gently but firmly up to the top roller and pin it in place to the extra supporting material. Use strong pins and continue to pin and adjust until the old fabric is quite taut and evenly stretched. Both the warp threads of tapestry and canvas-work embroidery are usually quite strong, so no damage should occur providing care is taken and adjustments are made gradually. The rest of the old textile will hang down behind the frame. Once the tensions of the old and the supporting materials are correct, put the side tapes on to keep the old textile quite straight and taut. Before beginning any stitching, check once more that the supporting material is slightly loose underneath the smoothly stretched old textile.

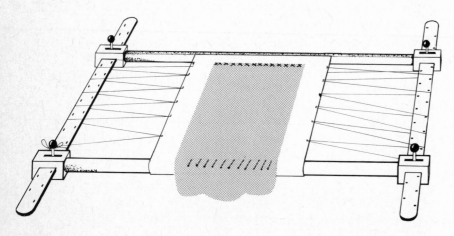

Obviously, once the area stretched in the frame has been repaired, the frame will be undone, the treated portion will be rolled on to the bottom roller and another area of supporting material unrolled from the top roller, and another portion of the old textile stretched for treatment. If the piece of old textile is small enough to go on the frame as a whole, make sure that it is taut and the supporting material is slightly loose before beginning work.

For the actual stitching, use wool to replace wool and a tapestry needle of a size to suit the thickness of the thread. We recommend Appleton's crewel wool, the individual strands of which are fine but any number can be used together to make up the exact thickness required. There is a great range of colour available and, if necessary, strands of different colours can be used together to achieve an illusive shade. Make a knot at the end of the repairing thread. Take the needle through the right side at a point three or four inches away from the area to be treated and leave the knot on top of the *right* side of the work, to be cut off later. When the necessary stitching has been completed, finish off by bringing the needle through to the right side at a point about three inches from the treated area and leave a length of unused thread to be cut off later. Knots should never be left on the wrong side, especially in material used as upholstery, as they will cause damage. We have seen knots left on the back of canvas-work which have actually worn holes in canvas and embroidery and have worked their way through to the right side.

If tapestry is being repaired, remember that the piece was originally woven on a loom and, therefore, a weaving technique of inserting the needle under one warp thread and over the next must be used when replacing missing weft threads. Never make a stitch which goes through a warp thread as this could cause strain later and would, in any case, have been impossible during the original weaving of the tapestry. A stitch through weft threads is undesirable but not so serious. Take all stitches through both the old and the supporting textile. It is when one begins to repair woven tapestry that one realises how necessary it is to understand how a piece was made in the first place if one is to achieve success in conservation.

Silk areas are treated by couching down all weak parts with stranded cotton in unobtrusive shades. We do not attempt any reweaving of silk. Any restoration work, however invisible and unobtrusive it is when done, is likely to become somewhat obvious as time passes, because the new fibres used will themselves change and a perfect match of colour at the time of restoration may eventually fade to something completely different. If silk areas are rewoven, this fact can become very obvious after a short time.

The highlights, around flowers for instance, can be successfully repaired by using Clark's Anchor stranded cotton. In the chair cover of a fine Soho tapestry, illustrated here, which comes from Uppark in Sussex and belongs to the National Trust, there was a blue sky area woven in silk which had almost disappeared. The conservation was effected by using a supporting material of a blue cotton poplin which was kept quite taut in the frame during stitching. The warp threads were sound and intact and these were couched down straight and even with blue embroidery cotton on to the blue supporting material. Small traces of the original silk weft were incorporated, wherever they had

remained, by being caught with the couching stitching. The result, from even a short distance, is of a complete sky area and, as there is so little that is new material, it is hoped that the appearance of the piece will remain unaltered for a very long time without the conservation/restoration becoming too obvious. After the work was removed from the frame, the parts of the blue supporting material which had not been stitched into were cut away so that there would be no chance of their pulling or distorting the tapestry above. This was necessary as the technique used had meant that the supporting material had not been allowed to be loose under the old textile.

In most pieces of tapestry used as upholstery, the warps remain fairly strong even if the weft threads have deteriorated, but sometimes warps have been cut or broken and it is necessary to replace these before anything can be done to replace the weft. To replace a warp, choose a thread slightly thinner than the existing warp and of strong cotton if proper woollen warp thread is not available. There is a kind of cotton fishing line which is very suitable or fine cotton crochet or macramé thread could be used. Thread a length of this warp substitute into a tapestry needle and knot the end. Put the needle into the right side of the tapestry about three inches below the broken warp end and draw it through until the knot lies on the surface. It can be cut off later. Bring the needle to the surface of the tapestry again between two warp threads and about half an inch below the broken warp end. Now insert the point of the needle into the weft and run it under the weft threads along the path of the broken warp thread until it appears at the place that the warp is broken. Grip the point end of the needle with pliers. Draw the needle, followed by the replacement warp, through gently. Next insert the point of the needle beside the place where the other end of the broken warp appears and run it through the weft alongside the old warp, bringing it out at the back of the tapestry about one inch away from the break. Again pull the needle and following thread through with pliers. Draw the replacement warp through until it is

firm and its tension is the same as the other warp threads. Take a stitch over an existing warp thread on the back of the tapestry to fasten it in place. If several warp threads have to be replaced next to each other, make new warps in the same way but vary the positions where you insert the needle, either making them nearer or further away from the breaks in the warps, so that the double thickness of warps does not become obvious. Always be careful to pull or push the needle exactly in line with the existing warps so that there is as little damage to the surrounding weft as possible, as the whole area could well be very fragile. Be especially careful to replace the warps correctly so that the broken ends which you join really do belong to the same original warp. If this is not done, there might be an odd end at one side of a hole and any subsequent reweaving will not be straight and will be visually disturbing. If there is a missing area at the edge of a piece, as could well happen on the cover taken from a piece of furniture, then make new warps stretching from the tapestry and anchor them to the linen supporting fabric at the other end. Sew down any short broken warp ends on to the linen and repair over these to cover them and supply the missing area of tapestry.

Canvas-work embroidery covers for chair seats, backs and arms, and for stool tops, are probably the most usual of all upholstery covers which might be restored at home. Having removed the pieces, made templates of them, and washed and dried them in shape, the amount of repair needed can then be seen. Frame up washed scrim in the way described for framing linen used to support tapestry.

Scrim is strong and open in weave and very suitable for supporting canvas-work. If the canvas is still strong, the replacement of missing embroidery may be all the restoration that is needed and it might be possible to do this without using scrim as a support. It is advisable, however, to do the work in a frame rather than in the hand because the stretching back into shape that would almost certainly be necessary after working in the hand could cause damage. Canvas-work done in a frame requires little or no stretching when finished, and the less strain on the canvas the better.

If there are one or two strands of the canvas missing, it is possible to embroider straight through to the scrim to replace the stitches or, better still, first replace the missing threads of canvas with linen thread, rather in the way one can replace missing warp threads in tapestry, except that the missing canvas threads may need to be replaced both horizontally and vertically. This is best done by stitching through the supporting scrim after the work is framed up. If, however, there is an actual hole, a patch of canvas may be needed. This must be exactly the same grade as the original canvas and should be stitched in place on the wrong side of the embroidery, exactly matching the threads in each direction, before the work is put in a frame. This is very difficult to do without making a bulky area around the patch because of the two thicknesses of canvas and should be avoided if any other way of replacing the missing area can be found.

The technique of repairing canvas-work is almost identical to that of doing the embroidery in the first place. Using a tapestry needle, replace wool with wool, silk with silk if available or use embroidery cotton, and replace bead-work with wool or silk unless there are old beads available. Again, we recommend Appleton's crewel wool and DMC or Anchor stranded cotton. It is necessary to use exactly the same canvas-work stitches as in the original but it is often only necessary to replace the top stitch in cross-stitch, where the old one has become worn or broken. A few stitches in a weak area will make it safe and will attach the old textile to the supporting scrim material which must always be slightly loose.

Be prepared for all sorts of odd stitching in the original and fall in with them, whatever private thoughts you may have about the technique of the person who did the embroidery in the first place. It is surprising what a lot one can learn about the person who did the original work. In embroidery repair particularly, one comes into personal contact with the past. We once had to restore two canvas-work chair seats from the same source. Working on them we realised that they had actually started out as identically designed pieces but the treatment of each had been so different that they had at first seemed completely unrelated, not only in technique and colour but even in design. We felt that they must have been the work of two very different members of the same household. Each was restored and each, happily, retained its own character.

GOLD WORK

Many people possess examples of oriental embroidery with gold work. These pieces may be displayed as hangings or on screens and they become very obviously in need of attention if the gold threads become loose. The design is lost in a tangled jumble of thin gold threads and present a rather daunting challenge.

First, examine the piece carefully and, if the design can be discerned, possibly in the form of stitch holes, and the gold threads do not seem to be broken, merely loose, then the problem of making the piece look right again may be one of patience rather than any complicated technique. If the piece is lined, remove the lining, marking the top for its correct replacement later. If the background material, on which the embroidery has been worked, is in good condition, clean with a vacuum cleaner and screening, and put the piece into an embroidery frame. If the background material seems fragile or has any weak areas, clean carefully and then select a suitable supporting material, such as a piece of washed light-weight cotton in a suitable colour, and frame that up and apply the embroidered material to it. If the piece is too long for convenient working, use the method described earlier for applying long pieces of tapestry or canvas-work to a backing material in a frame.

Once the piece is in the frame, whether supported by a backing material or not, it will be possible to catch down the loose gold threads. It will generally be found that any embroidery done in silk will have kept well and be intact but the gold threads used in the embroidery will have been caught down with couching stitches which are often of a thin, soft thread which does not wear well. These breaking cause the gold threads to escape and, because they have been held in whorls and spirals, they seem to spring in all directions. Find a place where the gold is still attached and look then for the stitch holes nearby and work from there to restore the pattern of the gold threads. Entomological pins are a great help in anchoring springy pieces of gold embroidery thread until the proper place can be found. Try to make replacement stitches into the original needle holes and choose a thread as nearly like, in colour and thickness, the remaining couching threads. The infuriating thing is to end up with some gold for which there seems no place, which possibly means that a whorl or circle has been left out in the repairing, so pin first.

With patience, this is not particularly difficult conservation work, and the results are very rewarding, as the picture becomes tidy and the design clear again. Tension is important both in the stitching and between embroidery and supporting material if that is used. If the background requires some stitching by way of repair, do this as unobtrusively as possible, perhaps near or into the embroidery or in a way similar to the other examples we have given for supporting a fragile fabric on to a new piece when working in a frame.

PATCHWORK

Compatibility of different fibres should be considered if they are to be put together in the same object. Almost all of us have seen what can happen when fabrics, not only of different fibres but also of different degrees of wear and age, are put together in a patchwork quilt. After a few years, the patches of old material, especially of silk, disintegrate, while patches of new material or longer lasting cotton and linen remain intact and strong. If silk is used then it is best if all the patches are of silk, and great care should be taken of the quilt from the outset.

Protection can be given to those parts of an old patchwork quilt which have become split or have perished, by stitching pieces of fine net or washed crepeline in appropriate colours over the damaged areas. It should be possible to make the stitches necessary to attach the net or crepeline into the original stitching at the edges of the patches. Do not take the stitches through to the lining as this could cause strain. Net and crepeline can be dyed if it is not possible to buy the right colour, but they are both almost transparent so finding the colour that makes them almost invisible is no great problem. This method of applying net or crepeline to keep fragile and loose fibres in place and keep them safe can be used in cases where old fabrics need such protection, but these textiles must, of course, always be treated with great care and handled as little as possible.

CONCLUSIONS

All the treatments we have described for conservation or restoration involve sewing. Needles do, of course, make holes but careful stitching – always inserting the needle between, and not into, the threads of the material – is potentially the least damaging form of treatment and does have the great advantage that it is reversible now and in the future. There are other techniques used by professionals but we feel that descriptions of these techniques would be beyond the scope of this book.

Up to now we have been chiefly concerned with the care of old textile objects, but many people who find textiles interesting are also involved with the making up of new materials, whether in weaving, embroidery, dressmaking or plain sewing. Some of the work now being done will certainly be treasured in the future as examples of our own time, either for artistic or historic merit. Few people set out deliberately to produce masterpieces, but we have described how many and varied are the causes of deterioration in textiles and anyone working with them would be well advised to give some thought to the suitability and lasting qualities of the materials they use before spending hours in skilful work on an object which, by the nature of its compound materials, cannot survive for any length of time.

Even beautifully designed and executed pieces can deteriorate in a relatively short period if the original materials are of poor quality, are incompatible with one another, or have been put under stress or strain and not given adequate support. Much embroidery and similar work is, of course, done as a hobby or on a voluntary basis – a labour of love – but if one costs out the hours that are spent, one realises how penny-wise, pound-foolish it is to use inferior or unsuitable materials for the time and talent involved.

The time to make all decisions of this kind is, obviously, before starting the work. As with conservation, so with new work: think ahead and try to anticipate where trouble could arise and then prevent it happening. If this becomes an attitude of mind, it is really very easy. Anyone who cares for the textile arts and who plays even a small part in preserving our heritage, both of objects and skills, will continue to experience very real satisfaction.

CHAPTER SEVEN

Equipment and Information

With all appliances and means to boot. — SHAKESPEARE, *Henry IV*

TOOLS

In any undertaking, having the right tools and equipment makes for efficiency and involves the operator in the least effort. The tools and equipment of anyone undertaking textile conservation are usually acquired in three ways. First, there are those aids which one would normally find in the possession of any person who has dealt with textiles and is used to handling them, whether in ordinary household sewing, in embroidery, dressmaking or other creative skills. These tools would include scissors, needles, threads, thimbles, an iron and possibly equipment for special interests – embroidery frames, sewing machine, dressmaker's dummy, etc.

Secondly, if any conservation work is to be done, there would be additional items which would have to be acquired as they were needed. Such pieces of equipment might well include a special vessel for washing fragile fabrics, a piece of soft-board and some melinex film and brass pins for drying correctly, nylon monofilament screening and one or more embroidery frames, together with specialised small items such as tweezers, a magnifying glass and a much wider selection of needles, threads and wools than would be found in a normal household

Thirdly, there is the sort of equipment which a much more experienced conservator or a group working together would hope to own for efficient working. Here we would expect to find some trestle supports for embroidery frames, a large table or table tops which could be used with the trestles, larger washing vessels, a supply of nets, dyes and dyeing vessels, stocks of supporting materials, threads, embroidery cottons and wools, large pieces of soft-board, rolls of melinex and nylon monofilament screening and so on.

What happens is that one builds up stock and equipment as they are needed and we have tried to make out a reasonably comprehensive list to include most of the items in the above three categories. However, no list of equipment can be complete for the simple reason that, as each textile object presents its own problem in conservation, the solving of that problem may require something which has to be bought – or borrowed – for that special treatment. In the early stages one can improvise, but there comes a point when only the correct piece of equipment will do. Once it has been acquired, however, it can be used again and again in other situations.

The acquisition of tools for conservation can become almost an attitude of mind. The serious conservator will make a habit of collecting catalogues, not only from the more obvious places like embroidery suppliers, but also from craft shops of every kind, surgical instrument makers (nurses' scissors are very sharp and a useful shape; medical tweezers are very fine and sharp for unpicking; surgeon's needles are invaluable at times because they are curved and angled), and art supply shops (artists' brushes have long, soft gentle bristles). A true conservator never passes a display of tools, no matter for what trade or profession it is intended, without looking to see if there is something there which would be of use. In this way, one always knows just where to buy the right tools for a particular job if the occasion arises. The list we have given is one which we feel would supply the requirements for a great deal of work. All the items are proven in use but more could be added as required and, of course, all are not essential in the early stages of conservation work or for someone who simply wants to do a little conserving or restoring to keep a few treasured textiles safe.

Equipment

REMOVAL OF SURFACE DUST

Vacuum cleaner – must have hand-held attachment

Nylon monofilament screening – minimum size piece is one square metre with bound edges

Wash leather – to be used with anti-static such as Comfort or Softrinse

OR

Perspex No. 3 polish – an anti-static

Sable paint brush – for light dusting in crevices

WASHING

Washing vessels for small items – shallow, flat-bottomed in various sizes. Photographers' developing trays are very suitable

OR

Purpose-built washing table – made of stainless steel or other non-reactive material with drainage outlet

OR

Large sheet of heavy-duty polythene, assorted bricks, wood, etc. – for emergency outside washing tank

Supply of softened water or water-softening agent
Washing agent – Lissapol N, Vulpex or Saponaria
Nylon monofilament screening or net for support during washing
Supply of distilled water for rinsing – from chemist, not garage
Sponge
Soft-board
Melinex film or polythene sheeting
Brass pins

 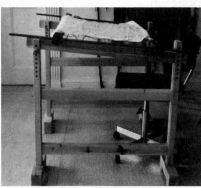

CONSERVATION

Embroidery frames – assorted sizes; if only one then with forty-inch
tape; smaller frames with linen centres
Trestles to support embroidery frames and/or table tops

At the Textile Conservation Centre, we have a system whereby
embroidery frames or specially made table tops can be supported by
trestles. The table tops are covered on all sides and edges with white

melamine. The tops are six feet long and three feet wide and, as they are exactly twice as long as they are wide, they can be put together on a module system, supported by trestles, to form the required size of table needed when lining tapestries or for dealing with very large textiles which have to be laid flat for examination or treatment.

Materials

Nylon monofilament screening
Melinex or polythene sheeting
Fine nylon net
Silk and polyester crepeline
Linen
Scrim
Clark's button thread in various colours
Anchor stranded cotton in various colours
DMC embroidery cotton in various colours
Appleton's crewel wool in various colours
Material for supporting old textiles is bought as needed
Scissors – of various kinds for different needs
Pins – glassheaded steel pins; brass lace pins; entomological pins
Needles – in assorted sizes; crewel; tapestry; sharps; curved
Thimbles – assorted sizes
Tweezers – assorted sizes
Magnifying glass
Measuring tapes and sticks – assorted sizes
Sewing machine
Acid-free tissue paper
Light-weight iron, ironing board and sleeve board
Pliers and other small tools
Hardboard
Storage boxes
Polyvinyl acetate adhesive
Small tag labels
Dust sheets to cover work

Documentation

Camera capable of taking close-ups for detail
Notebooks with pages for drawings
Pencils for use near work (ballpoint pens can cause irremovable marks)

THE WORKROOM

There is another aspect of conservation work which should be included in a chapter on equipment and that is the place of work – whether it is arranged as required or is a permanent location in a private house or a workroom shared by a group, possibly volunteers. No one can work well unless comfortable; therefore, warm but well-ventilated conditions with good daylight, preferably from the north, should be the aim.

Ordinary electric light distorts colours but a large workroom could be fitted with Philips 55 and 37 fluorescent tubes and then work can continue most of the year. Philips also make a good blue daylight bulb which is an enormous help for individuals working with a small lamp of the 'Anglepoise' variety. A sixty-watt bulb will be found to give sufficient light and true colour quality. It is also a great help against dazzle when working with gold thread, even in daylight.

Chairs should be comfortable. An adjustable typist's chair which enables a worker to turn round without getting up to reach for more thread, wool, etc. is a time and energy saver. Tables and embroidery frames should be at a comfortable height for working and should stand firm and steady. Embroidery frames are best supported on trestles because these can be adjusted to allow the frame to be at the most convenient height and angle. If trestles are not available, the ends of the frame should be rested on something firm and solid; it is impossible to do good work on an unsteady frame. Always keep work in a frame covered with a dust sheet, except when actually working – even then it pays to cover all the framed textile except the area actually under treatment. Be specially careful always to cover finished work which has been rolled round the end of the frame nearest to the operator so that it cannot be rubbed by the worker's arms while sitting at the frame. If the frame has to be put away between work sessions, always pin a dust sheet right round it so that it remains clean and safe while not being used. Never put anything weighty on top of material in a frame as this can alter the tension of the framed fabric and can cause sagging and stretching of old fibres which may not be sufficiently elastic to recover when the weight is removed.

If an iron has to be used, it should be a light-weight one. Set it at 'cool', but do not trust a thermostat completely and always test the heat before allowing the iron to touch an old fabric. Never leave an iron switched on and then go back to it expecting that heat will not have built up – it almost invariably does – and irons left switched on are a danger in every way and in all situations, not only when dealing with old fabrics. If the sole of the iron needs cleaning, this can be done with candlewax rubbed on the sole of the iron while it is warm (but switched off) and then rubbed off with a clean cloth. Never use anything harsh. Saucepan scourers or pads of the wire-wool type will make the sole look clean but they leave tiny sharp particles behind to rust which can cause damage to fibres later.

THE CONSERVATOR

No chapter on equipment would be complete without some reference to the one item without which no work is done, the conservator. There are no short cuts to success in textile conservation. All the processes need thought and take time, sometimes a very great deal of time, and a too-hurried decision or action can result in disaster, so no jobs should be undertaken by someone impatient who wants quick results.

Some of the sewing methods used to give overall support to very fragile fabrics can take a very long time to complete and it is worth watching oneself to find out the length of time one can maintain a really high standard of work at any single session. This varies from person to person or even, in the same person, is dependent on how one feels. Try to learn to stop just short of one's optimum time of good work so that all important work is done at the best of one's ability. Be warned, however: conservation work is very 'more-ish' and there is often the temptation to go on for just a little longer. Being tired can cause mistakes. We know that stitching is a reversible process but it is an unhappy way to prove it by having to unpick sub-standard or unacceptable work – far better to leave a piece of work which demands intense concentration until one is fresh enough to go on rather than push oneself when tired.

SOCIETIES

The following are a few notes of introduction to some of the societies which those who care for textiles might wish to join. Again, these short paragraphs are simply introductions – doors upon which the reader might wish to knock. All the groups cater for active and less active members and are not only for those interested in textiles or conservation.

The Association of Guilds of Weavers, Spinners and Dyers has about twenty-five branches which have regular meetings.

Information from:
>The Secretary
>Association of Weavers, Spinners and Dyers
>c/o 6 Queen's Square
>Holborn
>London w.c.2.

The Costume Society was formed in 1965 to promote the study and preservation of significant examples of historic and contemporary costume. It embraces the documentation of surviving examples, and the study of the decorative arts allied to the study of dress, as well as the literary and pictorial sources.

Its journal, *Costume*, contains articles by experts on the history and technology of costume and covers the whole field of the Society's interests. It is published annually in the autumn and is supplied free to all members.

Membership and general enquiries:
>Hon. Secretary
>Mrs Anne Thomas
>251 Popes Lane
>London w.5.

The Doll Club is an association of connoisseurs formed in 1953 to ensure the preservation of old and interesting dolls, dolls' houses and accessories. By organising exhibitions and displays of dolls, with lectures, expeditions, competitions and discussion groups, the Club enables members to share and increase their knowledge and to compare collections.

The newsletter, *Plangon*, keeps members in touch with each other and the activities of the Club. There are regional branch clubs in various areas. Applications for membership are considered every quarter.

Write, with stamped addressed envelope, to:

> Mrs William Garland
> Ashcombe
> Alma Road
> Reigate
> Surrey.

The Embroiderers' Guild, founded in 1906, is a registered charity which exists to foster the art of embroidery and to set a high standard of work and design. Membership is open to everyone interested in, or practising, embroidery and its related crafts whether professionals, skilled amateurs, students or the merest beginners. There are over fifty branches throughout the United Kingdom and a number of affiliated societies overseas. The Guild provides a resource centre, expert advice, portfolios of specimen embroideries on loan, a specialised library, classes and exhibitions. The quarterly journal, *Embroidery*, is for general sale.

> Secretary: Miss E. M. Haworth
> 18 Bolton Street
> London W.1.

The Fan Circle was formed in 1975 so that collectors and those who enjoy the beauty and skill inherent in fans could meet and exchange ideas, and hold lectures and exhibitions. The Circle publish at least two newsletters yearly.

Further information from:

> The Secretary
> Mrs G. Hardy
> 8/8 The Paragon
> Blackheath
> London S.E.3.

The National Association of Decorative and Fine Arts Societies, known as *NADFAS*, is a registered charity. The eighty member societies provide illustrated lectures and study groups of a high standard. Another aim is to stimulate interest in, and give aid to, the conservation of our national heritage. In 1973 the NADFAS VCC (Voluntary Conservation Corps) was established. The demand for more societies is increasing and interested people are needed to start them.

For further information please write to:

> The Secretary, Mrs. N. Mitchell, Woodland, Loosley Row,
> Aylesbury, Bucks.

The Textile Conservation Centre was set up in April 1975 as a registered charitable company to offer everyone – public bodies, museums and other collections and also private individuals – a conservation service for textiles of all kinds. The Centre gives training, in the form of recognised courses run in conjunction with the Courtauld Institute of Art, in day courses in preventive conservation, in short specialised courses for those in charge of textile collections and for exchange students from other conservation departments in Britain and overseas. There is also an advisory service on all matters relating to the safe-keeping and conservation of textiles.

Visitors by appointment only. Further information from:

The Principal, Textile Conservation Centre, Apt. 22,

Hampton Court Palace, East Molesey, Surrey KT8 9AU.

A self-addressed and stamped envelope for a reply would be appreciated by any of the people contacted.

FURTHER READING

A collection of books dealing with textiles is equipment of a different, but still important, kind. Books are part of the necessary tools for almost all activities. The list we have suggested for further reading is short, but each book we have chosen has its own bibliography and further reading can continue and be directed along those lines where the greatest interest lies.

ARNOLD, JANET, *A Handbook of Costume*, Macmillan, London, 1973.

—— *Patterns of Fashion 1660–1860*, Wace, London, 1964.

—— *Patterns of Fashion 1860–1940*, Macmillan, London, 1966.

BRITISH MUSEUM, *Clothes Moths and Carpet Beetles*, Natural History and Economic Series, No. 14, Pub. 55, London, 1967.

BUCK, ANNE, *Costumes, a Handbook for Museum Curators*, Museums' Association, London, 1958.

CLABBURN, PAMELA, *Needleworkers' Dictionary*, Macmillan, London, 1976.

CLARK, LESLIE L., *The Craftsmen in Textiles*, G. Bell & Sons, London, 1968.

COOK, J. GORDON, *Handbook of Textile Fibres: Vol. 1, Natural Fibres; Vol. 2, Man-made Fibres*, Merrow Publishing Co., Waterford, 4th ed., 1968.

GALE, ELIZABETH, *From Fibres to Fabrics*, Allman & Son, London, 1968.

GLOVER, JEAN M., *Textiles, their Care and Protection in Museums*, Museums' Association Leaflet No. 18, London, 1973.

HESS, FRED C., *Chemistry Made Simple*, W. H. Allen, London, 1955.

JONES, MARY EIRWEN, *A History of Western Embroidery*, Studio Vista, London, 1969.

LEENE, DR J. E. (ed.), *Textile Conservation*, Butterworths, London, 1972.

ROBINSON, STUART, *History of Dyed Textiles*, Studio Vista, London, 1969.

—— *History of Printed Textiles*, Studio Vista, London, 1969.

SEVENSMA, W. S., *Tapestries*, Merlin Press, London, 1965.

STOCKISTS

Supporting and lining fabrics – All fabric shops

Bump interlining – sewing supply stores; MacCulloch & Wallis, 25 Dering Street, London w.1

Crepeline – Pure silk: Exotic Thai Silks, 393 Main, Los Altos, Calif. 94022

Embroidery cottons – all needlework stores; Clark's Anchor stranded: Royal School of Needlework, 25 Princes Gate, London s.w.7. D.M.C. Corp., 107 Trumbull St., Elizabeth N.J. 07206

Embroidery frames – Royal School of Needlework; The Stitchery, 204 Worcester St., Wellesley Hills, Mass. 02181

Filters against ultra-violet light – For tubes and bulbs: The Morden Co., Harding Street, Salford M3 7AH. Anti-sol varnish: Lennig Chemicals, Lennig House, 2 Mason's Avenue, Croydon CR9 3NB.

Lissapol (U.S. Syntrapol) – Skilbeck Bros., 55–57 Glengal Road, London s.e.15

Melinex (sheet plastic coated with a mirror surface) – Percy Boyden Ltd, 5 Commerce Way, Croydon

Mystox (mothproofing) – Picreator Enterprises Ltd, 44 Park View Gardens, London NW4 2PN

Net – Wholesale: Black Bros. & Boden, 53 Stoney Street, Nottingham, or Picreator Enterprises, or fabric shops

Nylon monofilament screening (filtration fabric) – Picreator Enterprises Ltd

Perspex No. 3 polish (made by ICI) – Craft shops

Pins – Brass, lace 1″ ART FT 920: MacCulloch & Wallis. Entomological pins, size 3 continental: Janson & Sons, 44 Great Russell Street, London w.c.1. Glass-headed dressmakers' pins: Haberdashery departments, sewing supply stores

Polythene sheeting – Transatlantic Plastics, 45 Victoria Road, Surbiton, Surrey

Pulley and ropes for hoist – Yachting suppliers

Saponaria – Culpeper House, 21 Bruton Street, London w.1

Silica Gel – Silica Gel Ltd, Elvedon Road, London N.W.10

Thread, Clark's button – Most haberdashery departments, sewing supply stores

Tissue paper – Woolworths, or most stationers

Tuftape (made by Copydex) – Most haberdashery departments

Velcro – Most haberdashery departments, sewing supply stores. Manufactured by: Selectus Ltd, Biddulph, Stoke-on-Trent

Vulpex – Picreator Enterprises

Washing table – Frank W. Joel, The Manor House, Wereham, King's Lynn, Norfolk

Wool, Appleton's crewel – The Royal School of Needlework

General sewing materials – MacCulloch & Wallis; Abe Bloom and Sons, Inc., 137 West 23rd St., New York, N.Y. 10011

Other conservation equipment – Frank W. Joel

Other conservation materials – Picreator Enterprises Ltd

GLOSSARY

Alum – mineral salt used in treating animal skin and as a mordant in dyeing

Applied – laid on and secured with stitching

Appliqué – technique of applying decorative shapes by stitching

Basic weaves –

   Plain weave – simple weave in which each weft thread goes under and over each warp thread in turn

   Twill weave – weaving in which weft threads go over two or more warp threads and under one or more in one row, progressing along by one or more in the next row and by one or more in the next, thus producing a diagonal ribbed effect

   Satin weave – weaving in which weft threads are allowed to 'float' over several warp threads to achieve a shiny surface

Batten – a strip of wood

Bleeding – transference of colour from one area to an adjoining one by dye dissolving in moisture

Brocade – weaving in which a design is achieved by using different coloured weft pattern threads independent of the ground weave

Bump – soft, thick cotton underlining

Coptic – early Egyptian Christian

Couching – technique of laying threads on the surface of a fabric and holding them in place by stitching across them at regular intervals

Crewel needle – needle with a large eye and a sharp point

Damask – fabric in an all-over colour in which a pattern is produced by the weaving technique used

Felt – fibres matted together to form a fabric

Gimp – form of braid used as a decorative edging, particularly in upholstery

Gros-point – large slanting stitch in canvas-work

Jap silk – type of light-weight silk

Petit-point – small slanting stitch over one thread in canvas-work

Raised work – embroidery which is padded or raised above the surface of the background

Sharps – normal sewing needles with small eyes and sharp points

Stretcher – (1) wooden rectangular frame over which material, such as canvas for painting, is stretched. (2) removable side pieces of an embroidery frame

Stumpwork – form of raised embroidery, usually on a satin ground, much used in the Stuart period to cover boxes or as pictures. Scenes, frequently Biblical in theme, showed animals and figures, padded and moulded in the half-round or even separately modelled and then attached. Costumes, usually of the Stuart period, were of rich materials with sequins and pearls as realistic decoration

Tapestry needles – needles with large eyes and blunt ends

Template – cardboard or paper pattern made by drawing round the outer edge of an object

Tent stitch – simple slanting stitch used in canvas-work. Is also known as *gros point*, *petit-point* and needlepoint

Warp – threads, set up in a loom and running lengthwise, on which the weaving is achieved

Weft – threads going under and over the warp threads from side to side in weaving

Index